TACTICAL BRAIN TRAINING

A GUIDE TO TRAUMA AND STRESS MANAGEMENT FOR FIRST RESPONDERS AND THE PROFESSIONALS WHO SUPPORT THEM

Gina Rollo White, MA
Founder and CEO, Mindful Junkie

TACTICAL BRAIN TRAINING

Published by
PESI Publishing, Inc.
3839 White Ave
Eau Claire, WI 54703

Cover and interior design by Amy Rubenzer
Editing by Chelsea Thompson

ISBN 9781683737636 (print)
ISBN 9781683737643 (ePUB)
ISBN 9781683737650 (ePDF)

DEDICATION

I dedicate this book to my two favorite first responders: my mom, Adriene Rollo, and in memory of my dad, Tom Rollo. Their fearless natures, unwavering care, and enduring compassion profoundly shaped me, our community, and generations to come. You are both my reason why.

TABLE OF CONTENTS

HOW TO USE THIS BOOK

This book is set up as an interactive training manual for learning how stress shows up in your life, professionally and personally, and how you can relieve that stress by cultivating mindfulness. This book has been written specifically to support those who work in any type of emergency services, such as law enforcement officers, firefighters, paramedics, nurses, military personnel, 911 responders, corrections officers, clinicians, lifeguards, emergency room doctors and staff, and more. (To keep things simple, we'll be referring to this group collectively as "first responders" throughout the book.) However, the science and strategies in this book will also be useful for mental health professionals, friends or family members who are supporting a first responder on their journey to wellness, and anyone who has experienced some form of trauma or dysregulation as part of their job.

The book includes case studies, lessons, ideas to contemplate, stress-reducing interventions for use in personal practice and real-life scenarios, self-assessments, and resources, all chosen to help you identify your habitual reactions to stress and trauma and to retrain your brain to instead respond in a thoughtful and productive way.

Each chapter starts with a relatable story from a first responder that illustrates a high-level concept about the impact of stress and trauma. Following the story, we'll dig into the science behind that concept, then offer you some space to think about how the concept fits into your own life. Every chapter concludes with a mindfulness intervention that will help you experience the principles you are learning.

Each chapter of *Tactical Brain Training* follows the same outline:

- **Story:** Learn from a real-life first responder scenario.
- **Mindfulness/Science Overview:** Connect that story to an aspect of mindfulness and the science behind it.
- **Contemplation Questions:** Consider how the stories and concepts in the chapter relate to your own experience.

- **Mindfulness Intervention:** Practice a technique for regulating the nervous system and training the brain to think under stress. Each intervention is presented with the following:
  - **Written Description:** Step-by-step instructions for each mindfulness intervention
  - **Video/QR Code:** QR code linked to a video of a guided meditation associated with the specific mindfulness intervention
- **Self-Assessment:** Track your impressions of each mindfulness intervention to help determine which interventions work best for you in a variety of situations.

That said, this book is intended to be a "toolbox" for you to use in the way that best fits your needs. Depending on your intention or desired outcome, your learning style, where you are in life, and the time you have available, you may choose to approach this book differently from one day to the next. If you only feel like reading, go for it. If you only want to do the practices, just flip to those sections. Whatever way you decide to make use of this book will likely be the best way for you right now.

HOW TO USE THE MINDFULNESS INTERVENTION SELF-ASSESSMENT

Before practicing the mindfulness intervention at the end of each chapter, it's recommended that you complete the preassessment column of the chart to reflect on your current state of mind. *After* the practice, you can complete the postassessment and summary assessment columns of the chart to evaluate how the mindfulness intervention impacted your state of mind. Don't worry—there are no right or wrong answers. The goal of this self-assessment is simply to identify which interventions work best for your needs and feel best for your mind and body.

1. **Preassessment:** Note directly in the book how you feel *before* doing the mindfulness intervention, from 1 = you feel your best to 5 = you feel your worst

2. **Postassessment:** Note directly in the book how you feel *after* doing the mindfulness intervention, from 1 = you feel your best to 5 = you feel your worst
3. **Summary Assessment:** Note directly in the book how practicing the mindfulness intervention felt for you, from 1 = pleasant to 5 = unpleasant

MINDFULNESS INTERVENTION SELF-ASSESSMENT

Pre-assessment	Post-assessment	Summary Assessment
Overall Mood/Quality (1 = Best → 5 = Worst)	Overall Mood/Quality (1 = Best → 5 = Worst)	Quality of Intervention (1 = Pleasant → 5 = Unpleasant)

INTRODUCTION: CONNECTING THE DOTS

In 2017, with over 13 years of teaching stress management under my belt, I was in the formative stages of writing my graduate school thesis, "Mindfulness and Law Enforcement: An Effective Approach to Implementing Mindfulness for First Responders." Wanting to ensure my conclusions were evidence based, I began collecting data on the neuroscience related to stress and trauma. I was interested in how the brain organized information before, during, and after a critical incident. I also wanted to understand what occurred in the brain and body when someone endured critical incidents multiple times during a shift, multiple days per week.

But while there was a ton of information out there regarding trauma and stress, I was coming up short on case studies related specifically to first responders. Accordingly, I went in search of first responders who would share their real-life experiences on the job. I initially interviewed a diverse group of members from law enforcement, then widened my research to include fire services, medics, active military, veterans, and more to learn about job-related stress and trauma, as well as the existing framework for on-the-job mental health support.

The interviews were long and often heartbreaking. Everyone I interviewed had multiple stories of tragedy they had witnessed, experienced, or participated in. Moreover, they all seemed to be haunted by one standout story whose impact, as many of them put it, "sticks with me to this day." However, when the conversation shifted to strategies for stress management, our exchange petered out. While the toll of chronic exposure to stress and trauma was gradually becoming more evident, there was still scant acknowledgment of the need for support in processing this exposure. Some agencies and departments had in-house therapy providers on staff who reached out to employees (or to whom employees could reach out), while others didn't. Some had an internal peer-support group trained in crisis intervention; some did not. Established programs or formalized services appeared inconsistent, if they existed at all. Moreover, where mental health support did exist, it was typically offered *after* a crisis occurred, rarely (if ever) provided as a preventative measure. Rather than anticipating or acknowledging that stress and trauma are germane to the job, emergency response and law enforcement organizations seemed to regard mental health impact as a rare or unlikely occurrence.

With their employers rarely addressing or even acknowledging the importance of on-the-job mental health support, it's no wonder that most interviewees blew it off as "no big deal." Like many others affected by chronic stress and trauma, they justified the lack of support by persuading themselves that they didn't need it.

To an observer like me, this only made their pain and struggle more apparent.

Witnessing this widespread suffering among first responders left me determined to create a sustainable wellness program that could help manage the inevitable impact of stress and trauma on people in this line of work. At the same time, I realized that even the best mental health resources would be underutilized if these folks didn't realize they needed such support. Accordingly, I dove into research on the neurobiology of stress and trauma, studying the ways that chronic stress weakens physical health, cognitive function, emotional balance, and ultimately, job performance. Next, I looked at various tools for managing the impact of chronic stress before, during, and after an incident. Finally, I created a study looking at recurring stress/trauma themes and implementing tools for managing on-the-job stressors, rather than simply denying them until they become overwhelming. Knowing from experience that consistent and proactive wellness support could lead to better mental wellness outcomes, I was determined to support first responders in building new pathways toward peace of mind so that they can continue in this essential work without losing their health, their relationships, or themselves to it.

THE ESSENTIALS OF TACTICAL TRAINING

There are a multitude of in-house tactical trainings offered for the wide variety of emergent situations that first responders may encounter: medical applications like CPR and drug overdose protocol, firearm use and procedural law enforcement, and fire control and property conservation, just to name a few. These trainings provide step-by-step guidance for when and how to deploy specific tools, put on protective gear, and even use language and gestures with others involved in the emergency. However, I found no trainings offered, in-house or otherwise, for dealing with negative thoughts or emotions that routinely occur during or after their work. The humans involved in these events were left to process and recover on their own, often while heading to the next emergency.

After hundreds of hours spent observing and speaking with first responders in a wide array of roles, my takeaway was that to create a sustainable wellness outcome, a stress-management program for first responders must include the structure and features of other tactical trainings. Given the unpredictable and time-sensitive nature of first responder life (erratic responses to requests, long shifts, sleep interruptions), a training program must be interesting, user-friendly, and get straight to the point. The tools offered must not only be accessible at any time but also provide the user with choices. After all, while general tactical trainings can account for specific procedures in specific situations, an actual emergency is much less predictable. Since every crisis situation brings its own unique set of uncertainties, a training must offer a multitude of approaches, allowing the individual to pivot when necessary and apply or adapt a strategy to fit the situation. Finally, an effective stress-management training must look beyond the resolution of a single incident; it must be baked into every aspect of the job, as well as first responder culture in general, so that it becomes second nature to implement as soon as the need arises.

Armed with these insights and the data from my study, I designed a bespoke curriculum for training first responders in on-the-job stress management and trauma recovery. Unlike a reactive approach to mental health that ignores the buildup of stress over time and leaves first responders to scramble for steady ground after a traumatic experience, this new training provides tools for mindfully navigating the chaos and dysregulation they experience both on and off the job, teaching them how to prepare for stress before it happens and address stress while it happens. Just as important, this training addresses these issues without saying "you are broken." Most important of all, it works. After training with my program for just four weeks, participants reported increased sleep, better relations with coworkers and family members, decreased burnout, and renewed passion and motivation for their job.

That is the training offered in this book.

AN OVERVIEW

Tactical Brain Training is designed to bring out the best in emergency workers of all kinds. After working with hundreds of first responders and medical services and military personnel (and those who work and live with them), listening to their experiences and helping them find relief through stress-reduction practices, I've refined my original training into a program that helps first responders clear the collateral damage of stress and trauma from body and mind, replenish their reserves, and show up to work with their natural strengths—integrity, grit, compassion, excitement, passion, perseverance, and problem-solving—in full effect. Using the concepts and tools of tactical brain training (TBT), first responders become masters of creating calm amid the storm, able to be with the chaos of their job but not overcome by it.

WHAT IS TACTICAL BRAIN TRAINING?

- **Psychoeducation on stress and trauma:** Understanding the impacts of stress and trauma
- **Science and practice of mindfulness:** Learning about mindfulness techniques and their efficacy
- **Personal assessment:** Creating personalized strategies for maintaining resilience and balance

This book is divided into 15 chapters that will each take about 20 minutes to read. Each chapter begins with a real-life scenario, based on true events (though names and certain details have been changed for privacy), that reveals an opportunity for mindfulness, such as:

- Responding versus reacting
- Awareness of self-judgment
- Listening to your gut (intuition)
- Training your brain to think

Using each story as a guide, we'll explore mindfulness concepts like:

- Real-time awareness (knowing you are stressed or angry as it is happening)
- Focus (identifying when your mind wanders during moments of chaos)
- Trauma processing (identifying and addressing symptoms that result from a traumatic experience)
- Emotional balancing (modulating between what is and isn't tolerable)

After showing how and why each concept works to train your brain's stress response, we'll walk through a short mindfulness intervention practice that can help you manage stress while on the way to a critical incident, in the moment of handling it, and even after the incident has concluded. These interventions include:

- **Orientation**
- **Anchoring**
- **Square Breathing**
- **Sensing**
- **Signals**
- **Non-Judgmental Awareness**

> *To help you practice more easily, each mindfulness intervention is presented through both a written description and a recorded video (via a QR code to my YouTube page).*

Every mindfulness principle and intervention in this book is offered as a suggestion. There may be a few that you love practicing and others that you absolutely hate. Some may spark a tinge of discomfort, while others may leave you feeling nothing at all. This is all normal—mindfulness is not one-size-fits-all, and part of this training is finding out what works for you and what doesn't. By practicing a variety of interventions, you will be able to determine which ones best serve you. To help you track and evaluate your training, I've also included a personal assessment at the end of each chapter. Using this assessment will help you sustain your mindfulness practice by creating a personalized strategy for your unique needs.

Although the principles and practices in this book are written specifically for those who work in various types of emergency services, they can also be used by mental health professionals, friends or family members who are supporting a first responder on their journey to wellness, and anyone who has experienced some form of trauma or dysregulation as part of their job. No matter how you use this book, you'll find that TBT meets you right where you are, with actionable tools that provide practical support for navigating on-duty stress and trauma.

The fact that you chose to pick up this book is a testament to the fact that you are interested in health, well-being, and growth—your own as well as that of the people who depend on you. I am so happy you are here. Let's get started!

CHAPTER 1

THE OTHER SIDE

"The universe is full of magical things, patiently waiting for our wits to grow sharper."

– Eden Phillpotts

In this chapter, I will address:

- How I developed TBT
- The fundamental concepts of mindfulness
- Curriculum overview
- Mindfulness intervention: **Orientation**

CONNECTING THE DOTS

During my thesis research phase, a police lieutenant asked why I was interested in stress management for first responders. He seemed skeptical that I could work effectively with a professional group that I wasn't part of. My immediate response, while true, probably sounded a bit flippant: "I think first responders are cool."

When I got off the phone, I turned to my husband and expressed my puzzlement with the lieutenant's question. "Isn't it reason enough to want to work with people who I respect? Why do I need a connection to be effective?"

My husband's face wore a "you're kidding me" look. He patiently pointed out that while I didn't need a connection, I do in fact have one: Both my parents were first responders.

My mother was the emergency room head nurse for Saint Joseph Medical Center in Burbank, California, one of very few trauma units in Los Angeles. When disaster struck, her ER was where the victims were taken. Every day, she worked with people who were on the verge of death or had endured extreme trauma or violence. Her responsibilities also included pronouncing someone deceased and then announcing to family members that their loved one had passed on.

My father was a firefighter and paramedic for the Los Angeles County Fire Department. He was on scene for motorcycle accidents, assaults, gang violence, burning homes with victims trapped inside—all sorts of horrendous traumas. If he was lucky enough to rescue someone, he would take them to the closest trauma unit and drop them off, never knowing if they made it or not.

I idolized my parents. They held life in their hands every day, their collective knowledge was immense, and they approached most things with a ready-to-go attitude. Watching them interact with the world was like watching superheroes in action. We would stop at every accident to offer medical help and pull over for anyone who looked distressed, from a child left unattended to an elderly person who seemed lost or disoriented.

Still, my family's hypervigilant way of life had its drawbacks. We always felt protected, yet at the same time, we were always on alert, scanning for disasters, assessing situations. Going out to restaurants or movies or shows was never very relaxing. Wherever we went, we were always required to have an escape strategy, to know where the exits were, to never have our backs to the door. If my dad said "jump," we jumped; if he said "duck," we were under the table in seconds. We were always revved up and ready to go, yet always prepared to stop—one foot on the gas and the other on the brake.

I'm sure it is not surprising to hear that constantly running at top speed leads, at some point, to a crashing halt. I came to identify this point as the "other side." It was what happened in our home at the end of the day, behind closed doors, when the carousel of emergencies finally wound down enough for our thoughts and feelings to settle in. On the "other side," mom became sad, and dad became violent. Something trivial would happen—we kids were late coming home, dinner accidentally burned on the stove—and mom would end up in the bedroom with the door closed, faint sobs drifting under the door and down the hallway to our bedrooms. Someone would cut my dad off while driving, or my sibling and I would get into a physical fight, and dad's rage would blow in like a violent storm. In the time it took us to blink, he would go from 0 to 100, throwing things, flipping couches, punching holes in the wall. We never really understood what was going on; we just accepted it as our "normal" and learned that to survive the "other side," we needed to take cover.

I always figured there was a connection between the stress of my parents' jobs and their moods at home, but I never had the words to explain it nor the education to understand it. It wasn't until that lieutenant asked me "Why first responders?" that things finally began to come into focus. Of course I was drawn to first responders—their culture was my upbringing, the lens through which the world had come into focus for me. Of course I was curious about stress and trauma management—I had witnessed firsthand how, even when a critical incident was over, its impact remained. I have immense empathy for first responders because I've lived behind the scenes with them; I've seen what life looks like when the self-protective shield is lowered. I intuitively understand that for these people, emergency response is not just a job; it is *who they are*. Identity inevitably shapes how we work; how we work, in turn, shapes us as individuals. And nowhere is this more apparent than in regard to mental health.

CHANGING THE QUESTION

I was speaking on a panel at an Officer Safety and Wellness Conference when an audience member asked, "It seems like first responders are experiencing chronic stress and trauma. So why aren't they asking for help?"

I get this question a lot. I think it's hard to comprehend that someone whose primary job is to care for others would have difficulty tuning into and taking care of their own needs. My initial response to the question was to validate that stress is indeed a chronic problem for firefighters, paramedics, nurses, police officers, 911 responders, corrections officers, ER doctors, military personnel, and anyone who is on the front line of support for our communities in times of crisis. Along with intense challenges like rescuing a family from a burning house, pulling up to a fatal accident, chasing a perpetrator down the street, or working a sexual assault case as a daily part of the job, first responders deal with on-the-job stressors such as enduring physical and verbal abuse from the public, witnessing domestic violence, working an overdose . . . the list goes on. All these factors can take a significant toll on the mental well-being of these dedicated workers, especially as they accumulate day after day, year after year.

I then brought up the all-too-familiar concept of **stigma** as a contributing factor in first responders failing to ask for help. Admitting any type of mental health issue can create curiosity among superiors about job efficacy and leave coworkers wondering about dependability, generating both real and perceived issues with job security. As a result, mental suffering becomes the elephant in the room—everyone is conscious of it, yet everyone ignores it.

Among the thousands of first responders I've worked with over the years, I have seen glimpses of appreciation for stress-management tools, but that appreciation is overshadowed by nonchalance when speaking about their personal experience of stress. Many on-the-job stories are told with distance and even disassociation, harrowing details offered in a flat tone of voice with no evidence of emotion. When I ask follow-up questions like "How did you feel about what happened?" or "How did you deal with that experience?" I mostly hear variations of the following:

> "I'm used to it."
>
> "I'm fine."
>
> "It's what I'm trained for."
>
> "It's my job."
>
> "I'm not that stressed."
>
> "I wouldn't exactly call it 'trauma.'"

If running toward chaos is a job requirement, yet openly recognizing this leads to negative repercussions for employment, it makes sense why no one is asking for help. But that day on the Officer Safety and Wellness Conference panel, something gave me pause. For the first time, I wondered if we'd find more answers if we looked at this issue from the inside out. Instead of asking why first responders don't reach out for mental health support, maybe we should instead be asking something like this:

If first responders have minimal acknowledgment of the impact of stress or trauma, how can they even know if stress and trauma are affecting them?

SHIFTING THE NARRATIVE

Right now, many departments and agencies do in fact offer some effective "in-house" mental health resources that can help manage stress after a critical incident or traumatic case. These include critical incident stress management teams, peer-support groups, psychologists, and social workers. However, these services are often underutilized for a variety of reasons. Not surprisingly, many first responders sense that asking for mental health support is perceived by others, both coworkers and supervisors, as an admission of mental instability, which translates to being seen by management as not being capable of doing one's job. And that's just the ones who recognize they could use some help. As mentioned previously, a lot of first responders don't even see the need. Throughout my study, I heard a lot of confessions of problematic reactions or unhealthy behavior followed up with rationalization:

> "It's no big deal, you learn to survive on less sleep."
>
> "Everybody in this line of work occasionally has a few too many."
>
> "Sure, I get down sometimes, but I don't let it get in the way of doing my job."

Intrigued by these responses, I began doing a deep dive into the source of this idea that living with stress is okay. I wanted to know, at a minimum, why stress is underplayed and, at a maximum, why there is minimal awareness and acknowledgment that stress even exists. I realized that it could be boiled down to one word: **habituation**.

When a person lives in constant chaos (e.g., during childhood or within a professional context), over time, the feeling of stress itself becomes normal. The more stress they experience or trauma they witness, the more comfortable they become with that state of being. Feelings of intense frustration, anxiety, or burnout stop being a cause for concern and become ordinary, even mundane. This gradual habituation to chaos desensitizes them to signals from their mind and body that they are overextending themselves.

In light of this habituation, it's no wonder that "after the fact" approaches to wellness are underutilized. Many first responders don't even sense a need for mental health support until they reach a breaking point: an unintended explosion of anger, a seasonal illness that turns chronic, a realization that they can't remember their last full night of sleep, a hyperdefensive attitude toward mundane feedback.

It's further complicated by the fact that for first responders, even the word "wellness" itself can be triggering. It can imply that they are sick and need to get better or, just as bad, that the job itself is making them sick. It also brings possible deeper implications of blame and self-devaluation. A first responder considering mental health support after a traumatic incident is bombarded by thoughts ranging from *What kind of psycho chooses a job that makes them sick?* to *Suck it up; be a professional.*

All these implications are so far from the truth! It takes a rare and special kind of strength, stamina, and critical thinking to focus when the world is falling apart around you, to sustain great pain and suffering in the mission to care for others. The problem is that constantly scanning for potential emergencies means your attention is focused on the external, rather than the internal. It's important to shift the idea that wellness is only for someone in imminent danger of breaking down, or that needing mental health support is a sign of weakness. For first responders as well as everyone else, mental health care should be regarded similarly to other survival needs like nourishment, hydration, and shelter—a normal and essential part of everyday life.

Wanting to shift the narrative away from blame, sickness, and brokenness and toward self-advocacy and awareness, I began looking at things through a different lens. As I gathered more information, I landed on four general questions that helped guide my research:

1. Can our daily environment have an impact on our ability to positively interact with the world?
2. If there is minimal self-awareness surrounding the impact of stress or trauma, how can someone even know if it is affecting them?
3. Can we change the makeup of our brains for better emotional outcomes?
4. How would this work in real time, when the shit hits the fan?

Eventually, I realized there was a single concept that could help create harmony between learning to identify the suffering caused by stress and applying a proactive strategy to process and regulate emotions, all while taking stigma out of the equation. This concept was an amazing approach called **mindfulness**.

You may have heard this term before. Many books have been written about mindfulness, many courses teach it, and many articles, news coverage, and studies have reported on the efficacy of mindfulness. A broad range of definitions exist, but the one that resonates most with me comes from Jon Kabat-Zinn. In his book *Full Catastrophe Living*, Zinn writes the following:

> *"I define mindfulness . . . as the awareness that arises by paying attention on purpose, in the present moment, and non-judgmentally."**

I always knew that reactions were connected to events, but now I know that through training the brain to think, we can connect with the actual moment we feel a reaction coming up and, by applying self-regulating tools, choose how we want to respond. Rather than blowing up, we can notice our system is going haywire and take an action to calm it down, which then allows us time to process the information and respond consciously to the situation.

In other words, mindfulness is about becoming curious about what is occurring inside you as it is occurring. Once you are able to notice what you're feeling or thinking, you can process the information provided by your emotions and thoughts, and connect that information to a plan of action. This helps calm the nervous system, the control center for mind-body integration, by creating self-understanding and fostering a sense of **agency** (i.e., taking an action on purpose). For example, if you notice that you are angry, just asking yourself *Why am I so pissed off right now?* will calm your nervous system, giving you space to then ask *What can I do to decrease my anger?* This second question enables self-control, which helps you effectively manage your own behavior and, by extension, the situation. No matter what the feeling is—stress, trauma, sadness, anger, anxiety—mindfulness meets you where you are, wherever you are, and creates a safe space to land by giving you conscious control over how you relate to yourself and others.

Having spent the previous 15 years in the wellness space teaching stress-management interventions, I had seen positive outcomes from training the brain with mindfulness tools and techniques. But to apply them to first responders, where mental health was regarded with so much skepticism, I had to not only understand why and how these tools worked but also translate their efficacy to a context beset by chronic stress and trauma. How could breathing exercises, listening to sounds in the

---

* Kabat-Zinn, J. (2013). *Full catastrophe living: Using the wisdom of your body and mind to face stress, pain, and illness* (Rev. ed.). Bantam Books.

room, or tracking sensations in the body make someone feel more calm in the midst of unrelenting chaos? How could these interventions be adapted specifically for the first responder lifestyle and culture?

WHEN RESEARCH MEETS REAL LIFE

My research initially focused on the intersection of mindfulness, the brain, and stress regulation. Scientific studies show a correlation between stress reduction and following a protocol of mindfulness meditations, so I gathered a focus group of first responders and tasked them with following a short guided-meditation practice on a daily basis for eight weeks. The outcomes were astonishing. People reported being able to sleep through the night again, to notice feelings of aggression without acting on them, even to process their day during their after-work commute so that by the time they came home, they felt ready to engage with their family and friends in the ways they wanted to . . . all from spending just 10 to 15 minutes each day on focused awareness!

As ridiculously cool as these outcomes were, I felt like I was just grazing the surface. I wanted to understand what was happening within the brain in relationship to stress. I became obsessed with the concept of **neuroplasticity**: the notion that by taking a purposeful action, rather than unconsciously repeating an unhealthy established behavior, we can literally rewire the brain for a new outcome.

Most of us know that, at some level, we are all a product of our unique environment and genetic makeup. I have always resonated with the saying "I am what I am and that's all that I am." But learning about the brain's ability to build new parts and discard the ones that don't serve us left me in awe. I felt like I was finally in the driver's seat of my life, not just a passenger along for the ride.

To take my research to the next level, I needed another layer that specifically included first responder experiences related to stress and trauma. At my professor's suggestion, I went directly to the source, designing a study around first responders themselves. In it, I asked questions like:

- Do you feel stressed?
- What is stressful about your job?

- Have you experienced trauma?
- Does stress and/or trauma have a negative outcome on your life?

While quite a few study participants simply said, "I'm fine," a lot of responses included the following:

- Dealing with the public is difficult.
- Coworkers create a lot of stress.
- Shift work causes sleep deprivation.
- My family does not understand what happens at work.
- Managing violence, death, sexual assaults, homelessness, and other intense situations is difficult.

Next, I asked:

- How are first responders being trained in stress and trauma management?
- Is there even a desire among first responders for stress-management training?

Responses included the following:

- Kind of . . . ?
- The stigma is heavy—needing help is not looked on as something positive.
- It's a lot of work to seek out and get mental health support.
- Yes! There is a high desire for stress-management training . . . if only there weren't negative ramifications for asking for it.
- Stress-management training is necessary not just after an incident but before as well.
- No stress-management training is needed. If you can't handle the stress, you shouldn't be in this line of work.

The job clearly attracts people who want to care for others, in terms of protection or safety or medical needs. Yet once an individual was working as a first responder, it was apparent no structure was set up to protect, support, or create safety for them. Inevitably, this made me think of my parents, two people who did so much for our family and our community but lacked the training required to psychologically process what they witnessed and managed daily—not because they didn't want it, but because it wasn't clear what that training would be. Contemplating the responses from my study inspired me to create a training curriculum that took into account the unmet needs of first responders: balancing emotions during times of stress and regaining balance once the stressful event has ended. I pulled together all my knowledge from my research, my expertise from the wellness world, and my time spent with first responders, both during my study and during my childhood, and within two months, I was standing in front of the sheriff's department of Alexandria, Virginia, leading the first TBT session.

AWARENESS + ABILITY = AGENCY

I will always remember a conversation I had with a law enforcement agent during the early stages of creating TBT. He said, "So what you are saying is, when someone is running at me with a knife, I should pause and reflect on how I'm feeling so that I can be emotionally balanced when I defend myself?"

The obvious answer is no, that would *not* be a good time to pause and reflect. Not only would you be really bad at your job, you would also likely be severely attacked. Instead, the idea behind TBT is the same as other tactical trainings: to cultivate functional skills in nonstressful moments so that, when faced with danger and chaos, the muscle memory created from the training can activate automatically, eliminating the need to pause and think about what to do next. The only difference is that, instead of training someone to safely enter a burning building or approach a potentially armed suspect, TBT is focused on helping first responders instinctively regain emotional balance and regulate the nervous system in the face of severe stress.

This training is accomplished through mindfulness interventions that refine your *awareness* of the needs and opportunities in any given situation and your *ability* to assess and regulate your mental state. That awareness empowers you to respond to the actual needs of the situation using your thinking brain (**prefrontal cortex**), rather than reacting based on an unbalanced emotional state using your stress brain (**amygdala**).

We will go into a lot more detail on the brain's various parts in later chapters. But in general, when your amygdala is engaged, emotional awareness goes right out the window. Emotions can spiral out of control, thinking can become disorganized, and decision-making is reduced to whatever feels familiar and comfortable—*What can I grab and throw at the situation?* This typically looks like reverting to old habits that were developed over a lifetime, such as protecting yourself by shutting down and not engaging with someone causing you stress, trying to make the situation better through people-pleasing, or taking a defensive stance and getting angry.

While these old habits may have created safety for you in certain situations, they can be destructive when applied reactively or in every situation. For example, my mother thought she needed to look tough in front of her children, just as she did in front of the families she interacted with on the job. She hid her emotions, as if they were shameful; she needed permission to feel sad. My father, meanwhile, needed a container and boundaries for his frustration. He needed to be told it's okay to be angry, to be shown how to notice and manage it, and to be provided with a healthy outlet for it.

Old habits can easily rear their ugly heads when mental resources are down. But TBT helps us make the change from familiar but unhelpful reactions to new and helpful responses:

- When you train your awareness, either while practicing a mindfulness intervention or during the actual moment of chaos, the mind begins to reorganize away from habitual reactive states and toward cognitive responsive states—you know what's going down while it's going down (i.e., you can see that you are being a jerk in the moment of yelling at a family member or coworker).
- By training yourself to apply a mindfulness intervention in moments of stress, you build capacity for control over your responses—that is, you can shift yourself from an unfavorable state (stressed, crazed, sad, out of the zone, distracted, disconnected, detached) to a state of emotional balance and agency. Even while feeling anger, frustration, or pain, you remain able to interact with the world in a way that serves you and those around you. While this does not mean all your decisions will have the perfect outcome, it does mean that you approach stressful situations with a thought-out, composed mindset.

It might all seem pretty basic: Learn how to figure out when you're losing your cool, and then stop losing your cool. But wait, there's more! TBT also increases your ability to:

- Manage the chaos of work life (and home life)

- Be more present, with magnified awareness of yourself and others
- Notice thoughts and emotions as they arise
- Recognize triggers that provoke major reactions to minor issues
- Identify negative habits and replace them with positive habits
- Stay in control of your emotions
- Evaluate your performance without judging yourself
- Listen to your gut feelings
- Change your relationship with stress
- Find balance in life

WHY MINDFULNESS MATTERS

What: Enhances awareness of how thoughts and emotions affect the body
Outcome: Leads to better emotional regulation

What: Reduces stress and anxiety
Outcome: Limits the production of stress hormones that can inhibit neural connections

What: Increases ability to focus attention
Outcome: Boosts the ability to learn new information

What: Improves overall mental clarity
Outcome: Can help increase creative thinking and problem-solving abilities

What: Builds neural connections
Outcome: Stimulates growth of new neural connections and strengthens existing ones

What: Promotes better emotional resilience
Outcome: Makes it easier to cope with future stressful situations

You may be thinking, *Can all this* really *happen from doing brain-body exercises? And do I* really *need it?* My answer is that you'll never know how much TBT helps, or simply how good it feels, if you don't give it a try. You don't need any special knowledge, skill, or even comfort with mindfulness to get started. The first step in this training is establishing where you are right now. So let's do this by answering the first set of contemplation questions. Here we go.

CONTEMPLATION QUESTIONS

Take a moment (or more) to consider the following questions, then write down your answers in the spaces provided. What piqued your curiosity in TBT?

____

____

____

____

____

What were your primary motivations for wanting to train your brain for better health outcomes?

____

____

____

____

____

What is your connection to/interest in first responders/veterans/helping professions?

____

____

____

____

____

Now we get to the fun part, the part where the book work is over and your internal work begins. But before we dive into the mindfulness interventions, we'll begin with an orientation exercise that prepares you for practicing the interventions in later chapters.

Mindfulness Intervention

ORIENTATION

This initial setup tells your brain and body that it's time to practice mindfulness. In doing so, it helps your mind prepare, which then creates some clarity on what's to come. This also establishes a sense of ease and comfort for the practice itself.

How to Practice

Set a timer for practicing or do what feels comfortable for you.

1. **Before you start a mindfulness intervention.** It's important to orient yourself to your current situation. This means taking a moment to gather yourself, acknowledging your internal and external surroundings, as a way of creating comfort. Orienting yourself can help settle thoughts and prepare your brain for the training.
2. **How to orient.** After you have found a comfortable position, begin to think about where you are right now. Bring to mind things like the time of day, day of the week/month, time of year/season. You can also think about your environment and surroundings. What does the room look like? Where are the doors and windows located? Where might sounds come from (down the hall, outside the door, computers, lights, refrigerator)?
3. **Quick scan.** This process does not have to take long. It's a quick scan that is meant to create some immediate awareness and to create a sense of safety while practicing a mindfulness intervention. For example, identifying the location of a door may change your orientation to the door—you may choose to face a door, rather than have your back to it. You know that it's already cold in the room, so it's not shocking when you feel a chill. You see that the window is open, so when sounds come in, you remember why. The idea is to build structure before you meditate, which can help create a sense of security while you meditate.

Think of Orientation as a brief safety check prior to takeoff. It allows you to bring awareness to potential distractions or discomforts—the sound of someone talking down the hall, a sudden itch at the end of your nose, or even the vibration of a window as a car drives by—so that you are not thrown off by them. Proactively assessing your internal and external environment helps to prepare the mind and body for receptivity to the upcoming training.

CHAPTER 2

FIRST RESPONDERS, MINDFULNESS, AND STRESS

"The beginning is the most important part of the work."

– Plato

In this chapter, I will address:

- Adam's story of letting his emotions affect his work
- The concept of stress
- How mindfulness helps regulate and balance emotions
- Mindfulness intervention: **Anchoring**

ADAM LOSES HIS COOL

Adam looked noticeably sleep-deprived when he sat down to talk with me. He'd had a restless night with more up time than down. Was it the late afternoon coffee, or was it stress? Maybe it was both, he decided. He explained that every time he was just about to fall asleep, his mind traveled back to work, specifically to his last call of the night, which had ended with a victim being murdered. This situation was made even more gruesome by the fact that two young children had witnessed the entire incident.

Adam spent the night running through the scene on an endless loop, nodding off only to jerk awake at the memory of the children sitting on the curb, completely breaking down after seeing such a tragic event. He could see their pain, and it broke his heart. He recalled that he finally gave up the fight around 3:30 a.m. and decided to get out of bed.

Unfortunately for Adam, this pattern was a common occurrence. His first few hours after waking were typically fine, but by 7:00 a.m., just as the rest of the house began stirring, fatigue would begin to set in. On this particular morning, he recalled that things seemed more hectic than usual. His teenage daughter woke up late and in a cranky mood—which, Adam said ruefully, was more common than not these days. After rifling through the fridge and cupboards, she aggressively complained, "There is no food—what am I supposed to have for breakfast?"

This was when Adam started to lose his cool. After meticulously listing every single food item that was in the house, he followed up with a tirade about how his daughter was fully capable of shopping herself and, in fact, could get a job and contribute rather than complain. After some arguing, everyone left the house and went about their days.

Rolling into work a little late, Adam was immediately confronted by a pile of reports to go over. All he wanted was to get just one report done so he could get on with the day. His partner, Jane, walked in; he gave her a side nod without looking up. She said something, but Adam's head was down, deep in the report, and it didn't quite register. She repeated it, which annoyed Adam. Wasn't it obvious he was working and trying to focus? Looking up in frustration, he demanded, "What? What do you want? I'm busy—can't it wait?"

As soon as the harsh words left his mouth, he realized his error. His partner was standing by his side with a steaming Styrofoam cup in her hands. "Good morning to you too," she said. "I thought you could use a cup of coffee."

Reactions like Adam's don't happen in a vacuum, with no precursor. It's typically not one specific incident that sends us spinning out of control, but the accumulation of stressors that send us over the edge. Adam was exhausted from lack of sleep, still frazzled from his morning argument with his daughter, stressed about the workload that was piling up, and to top it all off, he still could not stop thinking about those kids sitting on the curb, forever destroyed by what they had seen. Adam's stress that day had built and built until finally the scales tipped, and he found himself yelling at his partner when he should have been saying "thank you."

There is a concept called the **window of tolerance**, coined by psychiatrist Dr. Daniel Siegel in his book *The Developing Mind*, that describes different states of stimulation and how they can affect the way we relate to everyday life.* When life is running smoothly, emotions are easier to manage. But when a chaotic situation arises, or we feel overly stressed, our minds revert to behaviors that may seem protective but can actually be harmful. The following diagram is an overview of what the different emotional states are, and how a buildup of stress and trauma can affect our ability to balance them.

How Trauma Can Affect Your Window of Tolerance

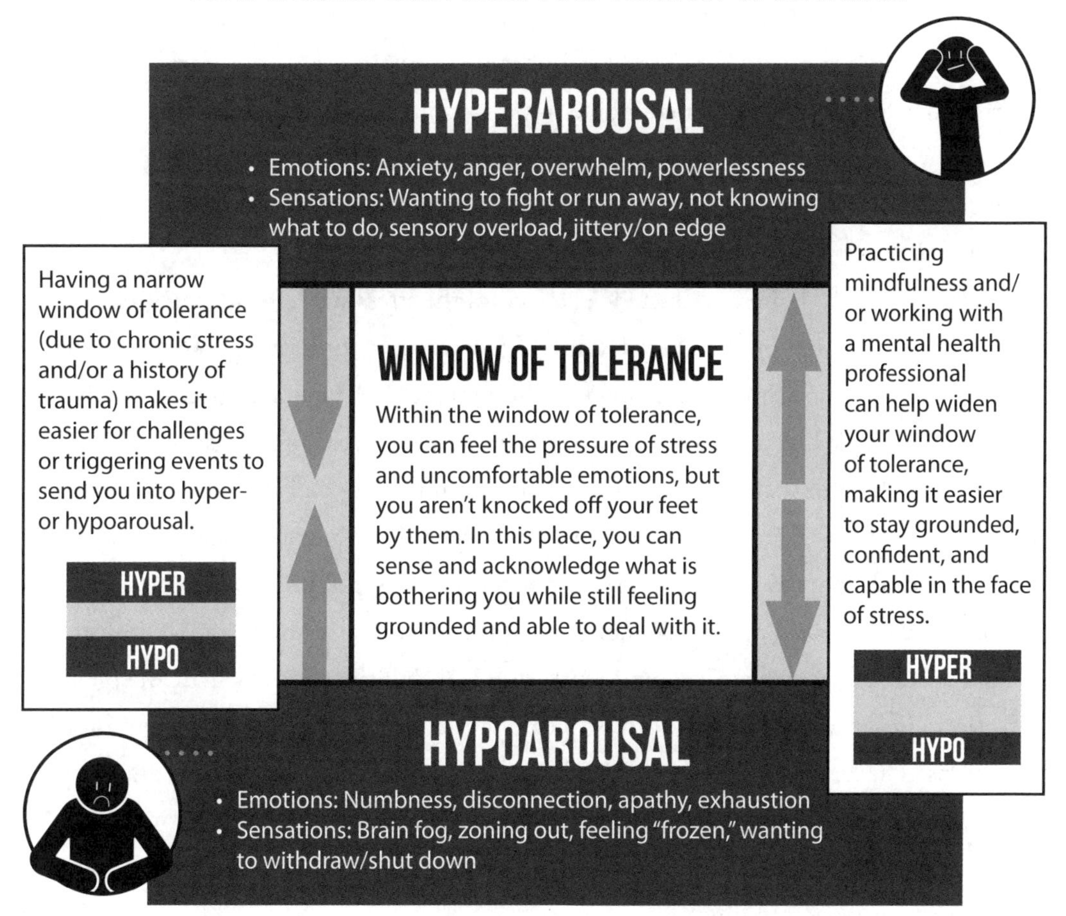

In Adam's example, hitting his limit for stressful stimulation put him outside his window of tolerance. With his mental resources depleted and his emotions out of balance, he ended up in a state of **hyperarousal** that caused him to translate his

---

* Siegel, D. J. (2020). *The developing mind: How relationships and the brain interact to shape who we are* (3rd ed.). Guilford Press.

partner's greeting as a jarring interruption. He recalled a feeling of vibration building up inside his body, and he reflexively lashed out.

This was not a new outcome for Adam. His family had expressed in the past that they often walked on eggshells around him. At work, he had a track record for snapping at people when his workload was high—in fact, he was known around the office as "Outburst Adam."

TWO SIDES OF THE STRESS COIN

Stress is part of the first responder experience, no two ways about it. But stress is not always the bad guy. It gets the blood pumping, puts the body on alert, and can sharpen our focus, making us better able to protect ourselves and others. Good stress helps get you out of bed in the morning, finish a project, or complete an assignment. It pushes you to work out, encourages you to reach goals, and propels you to take action in an emergency.

Still, even though there are beneficial effects of the stress state, the feeling itself can make the small irritations of everyday life feel downright threatening. When overly stressed, a simple miscommunication feels like intentional sabotage. A constructive criticism can look like a personal attack. An animated tone can be misconstrued as aggression. These misperceptions can send anyone into a state of distress, knowingly or unknowingly, with emotions that range from feelings of violence, anger, and chaos (**hyperarousal**) to distraction, sadness, and withdrawal (**hypoarousal**).

Because it's hard (maybe impossible) to eliminate stress altogether, a more realistic solution is to acknowledge stress and work with it, using the good stress in emergent situations and regulating the bad stress to ease the suffering we experience from those situations. The key to this is mental regulation—knowing what is occurring while it's happening, then making purposeful decisions in the moment. Creating a connection between what and how you feel helps restore your ability to show up the way you want to, at work and at home.

However, working with stress is only part of the equation. The other equally important part, essential for first responders and those involved in chronically high-stress or traumatic environments, is a clear strategy for becoming aware of, organizing, and regulating the emotions that stress brings up. Coming up with a game plan to manage the two sides of the coin—noticing the impact of high-stress experiences *and* learning to regulate response to that impact before, during, and after times of crisis—is what TBT is all about. It develops your ability to think about your thoughts and emotions in real time, as they are happening, so that you can respond in ways that help situations rather than make them worse. Each mindfulness intervention practice builds the "muscles" of self-awareness and behavioral control—you're training your brain to recognize you are doing something while you are doing it. Then TBT takes it one step further: Rather than just acknowledging that you lost your cool (*Crap, I did it again!*), TBT teaches you to notice the next time it occurs (*This is what it feels like when I'm losing my cool*), then deploy an intervention that helps you regain emotional balance.

What is emotional balance? While it looks different for every person and for every situation, in general it refers to the ability to manage whatever situation comes up without becoming overwhelmed by the associated feelings. Often described with phrases like "being in the zone" or "finding flow state," emotional balance is a feeling of calm awareness and mental stability. For the purposes of this book, we will define emotional balance as *being mentally energized and at ease, having agency and ability to rationally respond to situations.*

When life feels like all is going well, emotional balance is easy to achieve. But when we're feeling stressed or overwhelmed, emotional balance becomes difficult to access. When shit hits the fan, emotions fly everywhere like shrapnel, unless we bring our thinking brain into the equation.

THE FOUR ELEMENTS OF MINDFULNESS

As I mentioned in the last chapter, the definition of mindfulness I resonate most with is by Jon Kabat-Zinn:

> "Mindfulness [is] **awareness** that arises by
> **paying attention** on purpose,
> in the **present moment,**
> and **non-judgmentally**."

Let's break it down a bit:

- **Awareness:** Being conscious of the fact that you are doing something
- **Paying attention:** Deciding to identify and notice thoughts/actions
- **Present moment:** Doing it right here, right now
- **Non-judgmentally:** Without beating yourself up

Mindfulness teaches us to strategically think about the information offered by our emotions. It starts with noticing what is occurring at the moment it is happening, becoming curious about the feelings associated with what we notice, and concludes with choosing an action to ease those feelings.

For example, I was walking down the street, not a care in the world, when suddenly I felt "off." Because I have been training my brain for years, I quickly realized I had had a mood shift (**awareness**). I then deliberately became curious, wanting to understand what this mood shift was (**paying attention**), and I decided to do it right then and there (**present moment**). Rather than getting caught up in the fact that I was in a bad mood all of a sudden (**non-judgmentally**), I instead deployed a mindfulness intervention by taking a few deep, slow breaths. The intervention calmed me down a bit, which gave me a moment to identify more precisely what I was feeling and why. Turns out that I'd walked past someone who reminded me of my father, who had recently passed away; while I hadn't consciously noticed this similarity, my subconscious brain had registered it, and it had brought up feelings of sadness and agitation. Rather than getting caught up in those feelings or stuffing them down only to have them eat me up inside—both of which invariably make me relate to my surroundings in a negative way—I allowed myself to feel the difficult emotions for a few minutes (another mindfulness intervention that we'll discuss in a later chapter). Giving those feelings room to breathe was the final piece that restored my emotional balance and allowed me to continue on my way.

Through repetitive practice, your brain learns to **notice** you are losing your emotional balance while it's happening and to **take action** toward restoring emotional balance before you do anything else. This outcome is cultivated through mindfulness interventions. During a practice, you train your brain to identify distractions (such as a wandering mind) and gently redirect your attention back to a chosen anchor, like focused breathing, thereby regulating your nervous system. Regular seated practice prepares you for real-word scenarios, enabling your brain to learn the steps necessary for maintaining balance and agency. Over time, you will develop a preemptive sense for when your balance is about to go awry and an instinct for seamlessly incorporating a mindfulness intervention that helps moderate your stress and allows you to think clearly and respond the way you want to.

The tricky part, as you might have guessed, is doing this in the moment. We all know it's way easier to analyze a situation after the fact, but in the moment of stress? Not so easy. However, TBT helps you develop a sense for what it feels like when you're leaning toward imbalance. It's kind of like riding a bike. When you first learn to ride, you have no reference for how to respond to the bike's wobbling motion. But the more you practice riding, the better your body learns the nuances of the wobbly feeling. You develop an instinct for whether it's a "normal" wobble that will work itself out or a wobble that means a crash is imminent. You also develop an instinct for the right motions that will take you from wobble back into balance, whether it's to keep pedaling forward or to put your foot down on the ground and stop for a moment. With even more practice, you learn to anticipate what will create the wobble (a crack in the ground, turning suddenly, going too fast down a hill), and you automatically make the necessary microcorrections to avoid the wobble altogether.

In the same way, finding your emotional balance starts with noticing whenever you're out of balance and tactically choosing an action to restore your balance. To reinforce this effort, it's important to practice noticing without judging yourself. Instead of berating yourself once you notice that you've fallen into a hyper- or hypoarousal reaction, all you need say to yourself is something like this: *The negative reaction happened, I noticed it, now get down to business recovering the balance.*

JUST LIKE RIDING A BIKE

So how does TBT fit into Adam's story?

By the time Adam lashed out at his partner, he was already deep in an unbalanced emotional state. He was tired, his morning had been crap, and his work was piling up. (Sound relatable?) In this state, his stress brain perceived the interruption by his partner as an emergency. Having experienced an enormous number of tragic and emergent situations, Adam was primed to control the situation by getting aggressive. It felt comfortable for him, in the sense that he didn't have to think about it; he simply reverted to what he had done his whole life. (He mentioned to me later that verbally exploding was not totally satisfying; what he really wanted to do was take a swing at something.) After the fact, though, he felt horrible and berated himself for misreading the situation and not having control over his emotions. His reaction didn't just do a disservice to his partner; it did a disservice to Adam as well.

What could Adam have done differently? And how does mindfulness work in this scenario? This is where the twofold approach comes in: First, **notice** what's occurring emotionally (or physically), then **take action** with a mindfulness intervention that can help you manage the stress.

TACTICAL BRAIN TRAINING IN ACTION

Scenario: Adam realizes he just lashed out at his partner.

Mindfulness in Action:

- Awareness: *Wow, I just lashed out at Jane.*
- Paying attention: *What are my thoughts right now? What is my body telling me? Am I feeling any tension?*
- Present moment: *Okay, I feel really frustrated and like I'm losing my temper. My face is hot, and I'm clenching my teeth.*
- Non-judgmentally: *Yes, I lashed out. And I was able to notice it. Congrats to me for noticing what was happening!*

Mindfulness Intervention: *I should pause and take a moment to do some deep breathing.*

Broken down into steps like this, the process can seem a bit clunky. Again, consider what it's like when you first learn to ride a bike. You perch yourself on the seat with one foot on the ground, then push off with that foot, push down on the pedal with the other foot while trying to find the other pedal with your first foot, look where you're going and try to steer . . . and then, well, you know what happens. Everything feels awkward when you're just getting started!

But over time, with practice, all those elements come together in a single fluid motion.

In the same way, over time, with practice, your brain learns to recognize when emotions begin to wobble. Then it learns to self-correct before you go off the rails (or, if you're already off the rails, find your way back onto them). Eventually, you'll just sense when things are starting to unravel and, without needing to think about it, incorporate a mindfulness intervention to regain your emotional balance so you can move forward the way you want to, instead of letting stress call the shots. Just like riding a bike, mindfulness will become second nature—you'll feel like you've been doing it your whole life.

CONTEMPLATION QUESTIONS

Take a moment (or more) to think about what causes stress in your life. This could be work, or home, or both. Name your top five stressors:

____

____

____

____

____

DON'T FORGET!

Fill out the first column of the self-assessment chart before practicing the mindfulness intervention.

Mindfulness Intervention Self-Assessment

ANCHORING

The self-assessment chart that follows is designed to track your progress. This chart will help you assess three things:

- How you feel before doing the mindfulness intervention, from 1 = you feel your best to 5 = you feel your worst
- How you feel after doing the mindfulness intervention, from 1 = you feel your best to 5 = you feel your worst
- How you felt while practicing the mindfulness intervention, from 1 = it was pleasant to 5 = it was unpleasant

Fill out the first column of the chart *before* you move on to the mindfulness intervention practice in this chapter. *After* you've practiced the intervention, fill out the second and third columns.

Remember that these assessments are subjective. There are no right or wrong answers and no judgment. And make it easy on yourself—write it down directly in the book, and you can always come back to it for reference.

MINDFULNESS INTERVENTION SELF-ASSESSMENT

Pre-assessment	Post-assessment	Summary Assessment
Overall Mood/Quality (1 = Best → 5 = Worst)	Overall Mood/Quality (1 = Best → 5 = Worst)	Quality of Intervention (1 = Pleasant → 5 = Unpleasant)

Mindfulness Intervention

ANCHORING

This practice helps lay the foundation of the mindfulness interventions. It trains the brain to pay attention, making a connection between a wandering mind and bringing thoughts back to a specific action, such as counting breaths or feeling a sensation. It can help you recognize moments when you lose concentration and how to focus your attention on a chosen task.

How to Practice

Set a timer for practicing or do what feels comfortable for you.

1. **Find a seated position.** Sit in a way that is comfortable but not too relaxed. You should have a feeling of sitting upright but not "uptight." Allow your eyes to close or keep them open and focused on a single point.
2. **Notice your breath.** Bring your attention to how you are breathing. There is no right or wrong way to breathe; just let it happen naturally. Notice as your belly or chest rises and falls.
3. **Bring to mind an anchor.** Imagine a boat anchored in water. Then envision how the anchor works, keeping the boat steady. Now imagine the boat begins to drift and the anchor line catches when the slack is out, keeping the boat from wandering.
4. **Choose an anchor for yourself.** Your anchor can be anything you choose: a sound, a sensation, a thought. For this exercise, we will use the rhythm of your breath as an anchor.
5. **Stabilize your thoughts.** Begin by focusing your attention on breathing. Notice the rise and fall of your chest or belly. When you detect that your mind is having thoughts, return your attention to the rhythm of that rise and fall—it's the anchor that pulls you back to focusing on your breath.

6. **Refocus your attention on your anchor.** Thoughts will come and go. When you catch your mind in a thought, remember your breath is your anchor. Try not to get caught up in judging or interpreting your thoughts. Simply notice your mind has wandered and anchor your thoughts once again on the rise and fall of your breath. The idea is to notice that your mind has wandered, then simply guide it back.
7. **Repeat this process.** Practice for the duration of the time you've set on your timer, or for as long as it feels good to you.

Mindfulness Intervention QR Code: Guided Anchoring

You can check out a recorded guided practice here:

Mindfulness Intervention Self-Assessment

Return to the self-assessment chart to fill out the postassessment and summary assessment columns *after* you practice the mindfulness intervention.

CHAPTER 3

STRESS AND THE BRAIN

"We do not simply live in this universe.
The universe lives within us."

– Neil deGrasse Tyson

In this chapter, I will address:

- Sam's story of "blacking out" in response to stress
- Stress and the brain
- How mindfulness helps regulate stress
- Mindfulness intervention: **Breathing**

THE WALK

Sam was a corrections deputy in his 20s who had worked in a federal detention center for just over a year. The detention center was constantly filled with local lawbreakers brought in for DUIs and public disturbances, as well as more serious crimes like sexual and domestic assault. Because it was a federal detention center, it was also filled with those awaiting trial for federal crimes, from the heinous to the mundane. The duties of the deputies followed a monthly rotation: intake, transportation, male population, female population. But everyone's schedule always included at least one day on the top floor, which housed the violent offenders. This population was considered high risk, requiring special procedures different from the rest of detention center. Due to their potential for dangerous behavior, whenever a detainee on this floor was moved for any reason, the entire detention center went on lockdown until the transfer was completed.

I happened to be present during one transfer and witnessed firsthand how challenging it can be. A deputy was taking me to the kitchen cafeteria for my TBT sessions with inmates when he was called up to the top floor. Since he couldn't leave me alone, I went along with him. As we got out of the elevator, we were notified that a transfer was occurring right then. The detention center went on lockdown.

Everyone moved into action fast, and the energy level intensified. I could hear multiple radios instructing deputies to follow protocol. Inmates were instructed to either stay put in a secure location or head directly to their cells. I was standing near a doorway, directly across from a row of cells—there was nowhere for me to go. The deputy told me to just stand against the wall, stay still, and keep my eyes down. He then moved to the other side of the hall and stood at the door, waiting to assist with the inmate transfer.

I already knew whom they had on the top floor and why, and I really did not want to be any part of this man's story. In the span of three minutes, I tried every regulating breathing technique known to humankind while trying my best to disappear against the wall as he walked by, inches from my face. I consider it a success that I only had a small internal panic attack, rather than a full-blown freak-out. It's no stretch to say my visit to the top floor was one of the top 10 most stressful events I have ever experienced.

Sam was working the top floor one day when he was called to relocate an inmate from one cell to another. Despite the high level of alertness required, relocation is pretty straightforward if you are trained and have done it before. Unfortunately, this was Sam's first top-floor relocation, and he was on high alert in an uncomfortable and dysregulating way. The inmate he was transferring was known to be disruptive, manipulative, and extremely violent, both on the outside and within the detention center. Sam recalled feeling "jacked up" (his words) before he even opened the cell door.

After they began walking—inmate in front, Sam behind—the inmate made a jerking motion, tripped a bit, and mumbled something. For Sam, time stopped. He remembered thinking, *Did he do that on purpose? Am I being set up for something?*

Then, what seemed like only a moment later, Sam was no longer walking behind the inmate but was instead looking into the man's very red face at close range. He realized he had the inmate pushed up against the wall, locked in a chokehold. Sam had no memory of how he got there or even of having made the decision to restrain the inmate, but with his thinking back online and the man's face turning blue in front of him, Sam knew he needed to release the inmate, or he would choke him to death.

STRESS AND THE BRAIN

Sam's story is a window into how stress and the brain work. Sam's state of high alert was a very appropriate response for the situation and was in line with his training. But things spiraled when the inmate made an unexpected movement. Sam recalled a visceral feeling in his body as his academy instruction kicked in. *This is the dangerous situation I've trained for—holy shit, it's happening right now!*

The question is whether what he thought was happening was in fact actually happening. In other words, was this a real emergency or a perceived emergency?

In every situation we encounter, our brain goes through a well-practiced process of receiving input, evaluating how important the input is, deciding which cognitive processes should be made available, then taking an action. Is the fire hot? Move hand away from fire. Do I feel dehydrated? Drink some water. But sometimes a decision gets made without all the information or with information that is incorrectly processed. For example, you're out hiking and suddenly see a snake lying in your path. You instinctively jump back, then do a double take and realize what you saw was actually just a stick.

Decision-Making

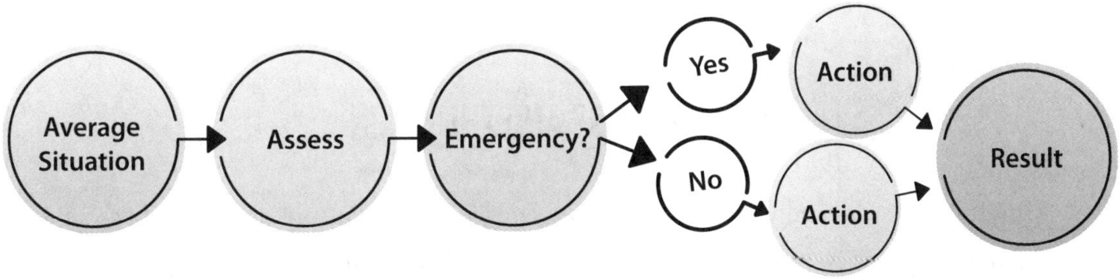

Average Situation
Assess
Emergency?
Yes
No
Action
Action
Result

Your emotional state while processing information plays a huge role in how the brain coordinates reactions and responses. It can lead to a difference between assessing something as a real emergency versus a perceived emergency. With the snake example, the thinking brain quickly makes an assessment based on input: *I am walking in the woods. I see a long brown object in my path. I saw this in a book once. Crap, it must be a snake!* Depending on your emotional state, either the thinking brain comes online and coordinates an appropriate action, or the emotional brain hijacks the situation with an emergency action: *This is an emergency—stop assessing and run!* Similarly, when Sam saw the inmate make an unexpected movement, his logical brain initially said, *This guy is doing something strange. I think he is doing something dangerous.* And because Sam was feeling anxious about his first inmate transfer, his high-stress state made it easy for his emotional brain to override logic, and he then unconsciously shifted into attack mode.

Under Stress, Everything Is a Perceived Emergency

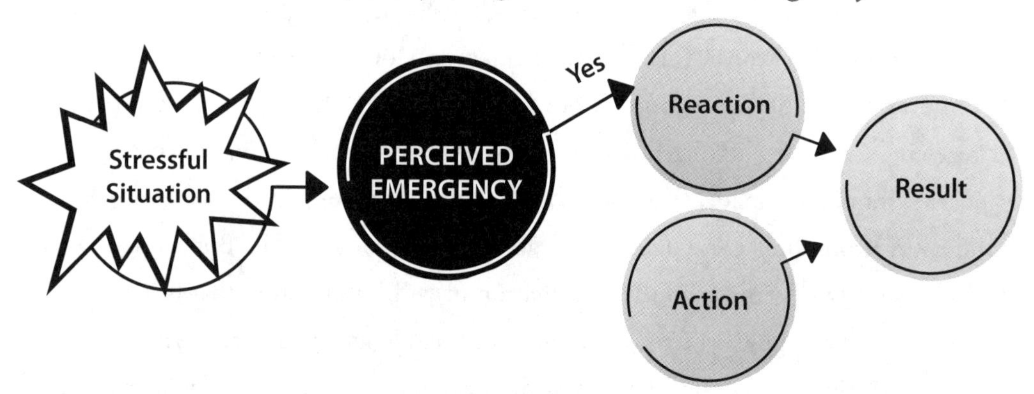

You might be thinking, *Better to react than get bitten by a snake or killed by some crazy maniac.* I definitely agree. But wouldn't it be even better if you could somehow assess and respond to a situation consciously and constructively, rather than jump to conclusions or react without all the information?

MINDFULNESS AND THE BRAIN

Mindfulness is integrally connected with agency. To build on the definition back in chapter 1, agency is the difference between **responding** (taking deliberate, thoughtful action in response to the stimulus) and **reacting** (taking thoughtless, unaware action in reaction to the stimulus).

In general, the actions we take are organized and drawn from various areas of our brain that are implicated with different functions, processing, and outcomes. For instance, we use the occipital lobe to process sight, the cerebellum to manage balance, and the temporal lobe to process auditory information and encode memory.

Different Regions Implicated in Different Outcomes

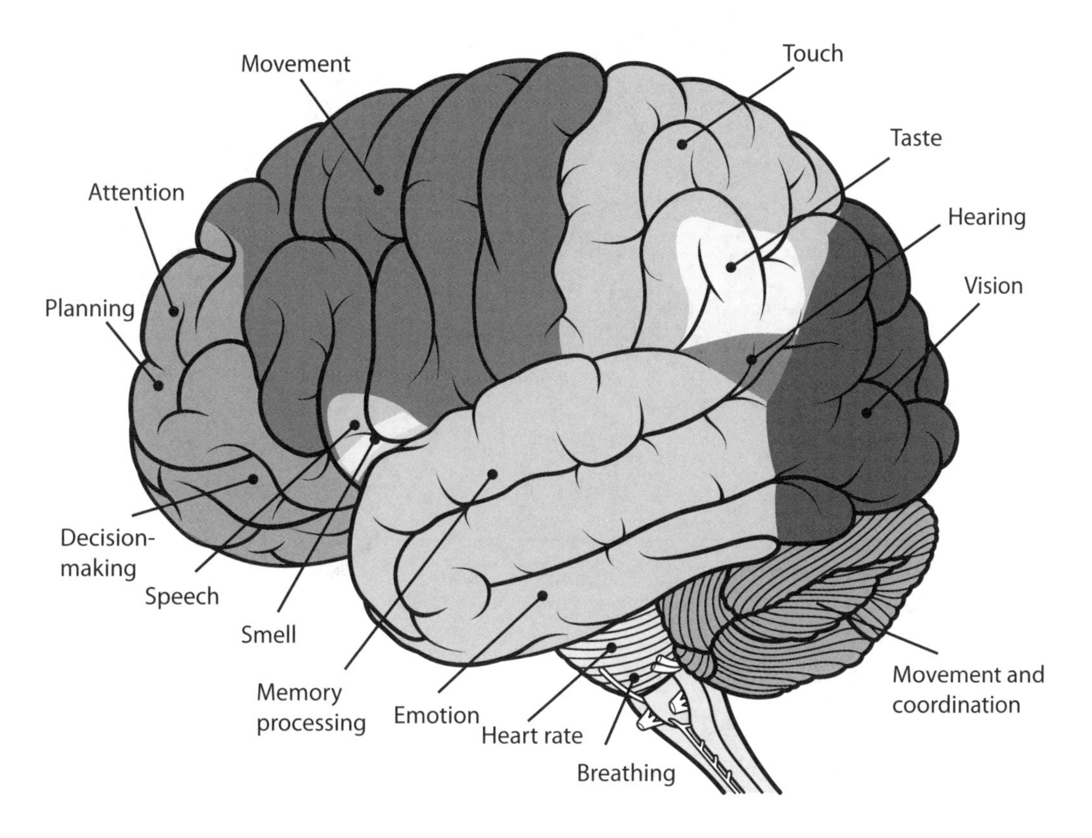

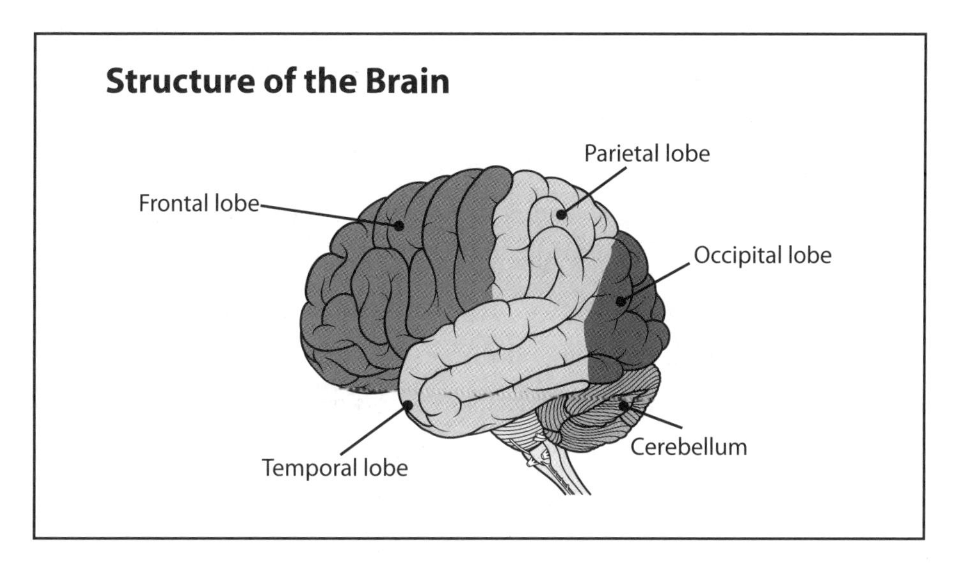

There are two areas of the brain that help us better understand the distinction between responding and reacting: the **prefrontal cortex** and the **amygdala**.

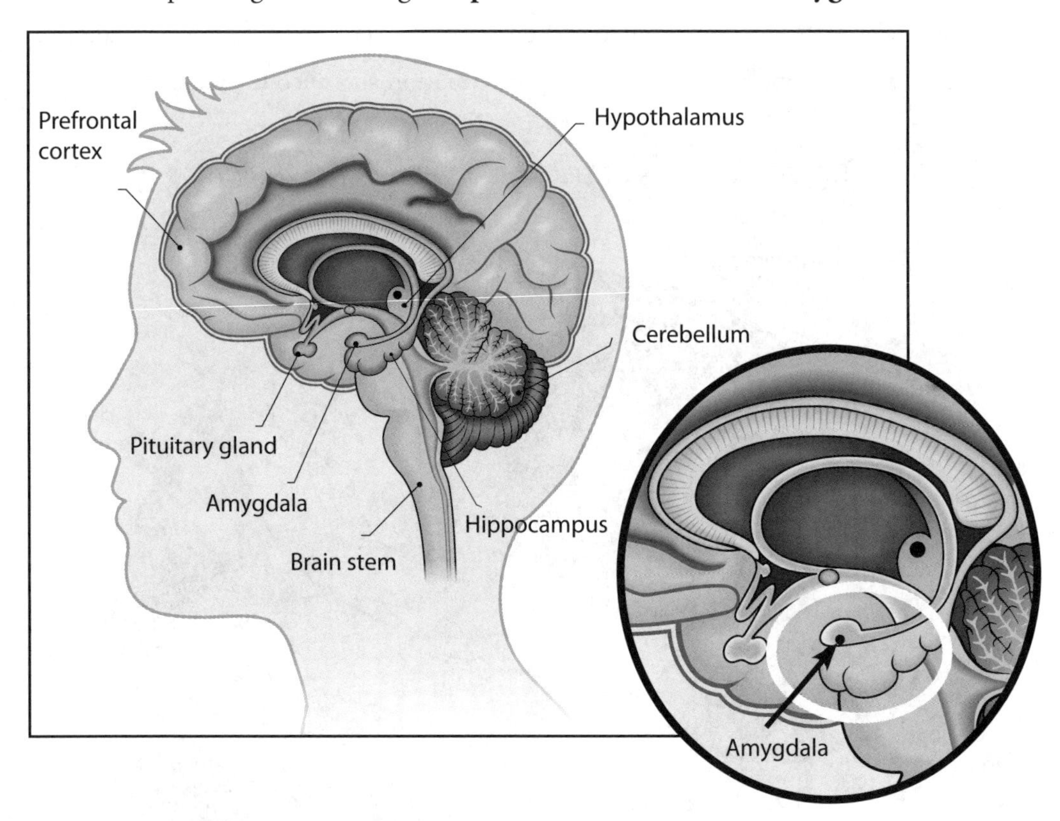

When we use our thinking brain (what neuroscientists call "executive functioning"), we are engaging the prefrontal cortex (PFC). Located in the frontal lobe of the brain, the job of the PFC is to process and organize information. Some of its basic functions include problem-solving, thought regulation, comprehension, impulse control, creativity, and perseverance. The PFC is what we want to tap into when we are responding to a stimulus—it takes information from the inside and outside worlds and taps into its memory bank for reference points, which leads to constructive decision-making about what to do.

Then there's the amygdala, sometimes referred to as the stress center of the brain. Although the picture only shows one amygdala, there are actually two of them, both shaped like almonds and located on either side of the brain. The amygdala is predominantly concerned with fear and threat. It constantly scans our environment for dangerous situations and, once it decides there is danger, sends a message to the body to take a protective action. Typically, this protective action shows up in the form of fight, flight, freeze, or fawn.

As you can see in the previous picture, the actual physical size of the amygdala is very small. But this was not always the case. The human brain has changed over time as we've evolved to our present-day form; back in our caveman days, the amygdala was much larger. This makes perfect sense when you consider how cavemen lived in constant survival mode. It was a dangerous time—just existing was a constant struggle. Emergent situations were around every boulder, creating a continual state of reactivity: fight (for things like food or shelter), take flight (from hungry tigers or other aggressive cavemen), freeze (hide or play dead in hopes that an aggressor will pass by), or fawn (attempt to appease an aggressor through compliance or submission). The amygdala played a dominant role in helping early humans survive these moment-to-moment emergencies with single-minded purpose and quick, effective action.

The following graphic helps show the contrast between our brain structure today (left) and that of our caveman ancestors (right). You'll notice how the caveman has a flattish forehead and an extended back area of the head. Again, the front part of the brain is the prefrontal cortex (the thinking brain), while the back area is the cerebellum, which manages movement, balance, and coordination.

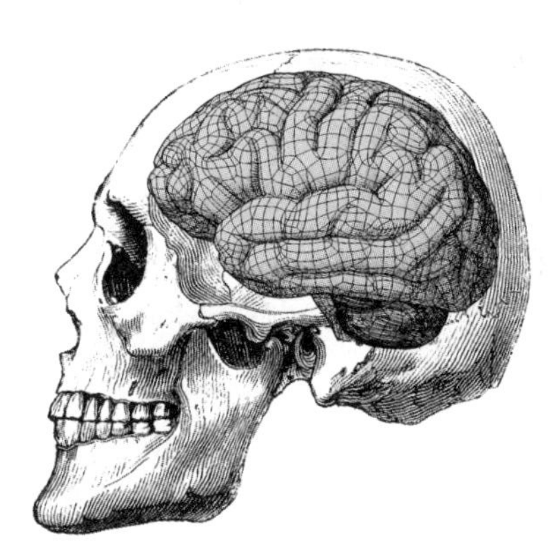

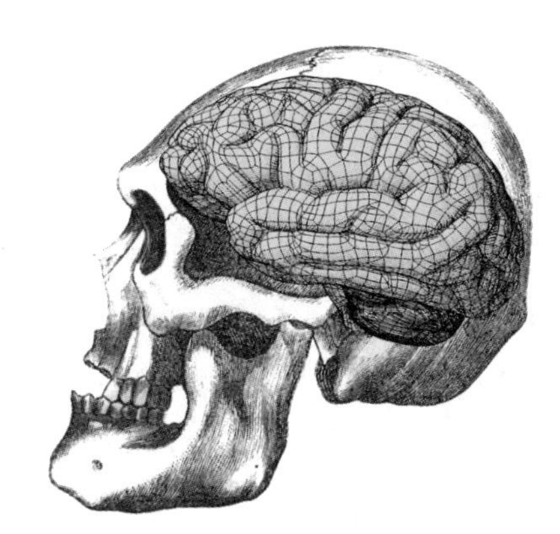

Just as with muscles, the more you use a particular region of the brain, the stronger that part of the brain becomes. This is true both in the lifespan of a single human and in the course of human evolution. Over millions of years, the brain changed as a direct result of use and nonuse. As immediate physical threats decreased, the threat-sensing amygdala decreased in size. Meanwhile, the more logic and thinking came into use, the bigger the PFC grew.

The modern-day brain has evolved away from survival-oriented reacting to logical processing and contemplation. For the most part, our moment-to-moment need to survive has decreased. Instead of running from the tiger, we now carry guns and build traps that make the tiger run from us. Instead of freezing from the cold, we build sustainable heat. Information comes in, it's passed along to the PFC, a logical decision is made, and an appropriate action is taken.

> *It would be wrong if I didn't acknowledge that strife and misfortune do still exist in today's world. Many individuals and even societies are currently struggling with immediate threats to survival, such as war, lack of housing, starvation, abuse, and many other atrocities. What I am focused on in this book is stress and trauma experienced in the modern-day life of first responders. I will leave the broader subjects to experts who can address those.*

At least, that's the ideal scenario. And when we're within our window of tolerance, this system works well. Even though it has evolved to be smaller, the amygdala still retains its job as a threat sensor. This distinction is important: The amygdala does not assess whether a threat is real or not, it simply notices a potential threat, names it, and passes the information on to another part of the brain called the **hippocampus**. The hippocampus is responsible for learning and memory. One thing it remembers to do is gather information from the amygdala and send it to the PFC, which decides how to proceed. The PFC then sends its decision back down into the body for it to take an action. For instance, if you see smoke coming from a building, the amygdala will immediately begin to let the hippocampus know it thinks there is an emergency. Assuming you are in your window of tolerance (not feeling stressed or overwhelmed), here's how your brain might react:

EXAMPLE ONE: NOT STRESSED OUT

Scenario: After a smooth morning routine and a stress-free commute, you cruise into work. While at your desk, you see smoke coming from a nearby building.

Amygdala: Hmm, I see smoke. What should I do?

Hippocampus: Seems like this may be important. I will let the PFC know what's going on.

PFC: Let me scan and assess. Okay, it's just some smoke coming from the factory at the end of the block. We've seen this before. No action required.

Now, here's where it gets complicated. When stress or overwhelm has heightened your state of arousal, the amygdala goes into overdrive. It's no longer "curious" if something is an emergency, it just assumes it's an emergency. Rather than asking the PFC what the body should do next, it instead takes matters into its own hands, goes rogue, and reacts to the perceived emergency by immediately safeguarding the body. The PFC has no time to provide a rational course of action, because the amygdala quickly jumps into action, treating the situation as if the body is facing an imminent threat. At a very high level, the amygdala does this by flooding the body with hormones like adrenaline and cortisol. Cortisol in particular acts like a military sergeant, getting the body ready to take action. (This is when you feel a rush of energy or strength.) When cortisol finishes its cycle through the system, it travels back up the brainstem and hits the amygdala, where the chemical reaction creates a heavy filter between the amygdala and the hippocampus. This results in minimal communication between the hippocampus and the PFC, preventing the information from being logically processed.

This approach is great when a threat is real. These hormones inform the body that urgent action is needed and provide a surge of energy needed to run, lift or carry enormous amounts of weight, or fight back. In the right moment, this can be lifesaving; again, stress is not always a bad thing. However, if this approach is activated when something is not a real threat, accurately assessing situations becomes difficult, and sometimes (okay, oftentimes) this leads to an overreaction. With the PFC out of commission, the amygdala steps in to "save the day."

EXAMPLE TWO: STRESSED OUT

Scenario: Morning was difficult, commute was twice as long as usual, work is chaos, everything sucks.

Amygdala: I see smoke. Holy shit, what do I do?

Hippocampus: [Crickets.]

PFC: [Clueless.]

Amygdala: SMOKE EQUALS FIRE. THERE MUST BE A FIRE. IT'S DEFINITELY A FIRE. GET THE F OUT AND RUN. RUN! *RUN!*

BACK TO SAM

Based on what we now know about the amygdala and the PFC, let's get back to Sam. Recall that he was already feeling highly stressed about transferring this violent prisoner even before opening the cell doors; the anticipation of potential danger was top of mind. So, when something unexpected occurred, his amygdala was already suited up and on the field. The result was Sam reacting without thinking or assessing accurately.

Here is where TBT comes in. First, TBT helps us notice what's occurring for us while it's occurring. Second, TBT nudges us to steady the nervous system by applying a mindfulness intervention. When the nervous system is jacked up, decisions are also jacked up; calming the nervous system provides the brain some space to process information.

In retrospect, Sam remembered thinking ahead of time that the inmate was going to do something violent, maybe fight and try to run. He recalled being startled when the inmate tripped, and since he was already dysregulated and not thinking clearly, Sam went from walking to restraining the inmate with no time in between. It wasn't until after he had the inmate in a chokehold that his mindfulness training kicked in and he was able to assess the situation accurately. Once he realized things were out of whack (to say the least), he remembered to apply a tool that could regulate his nervous system, allowing for problem-solving and thought organization.

TACTICAL BRAIN TRAINING IN ACTION

Scenario: Sam is worried and preoccupied with thoughts of the inmate becoming violent. While they are walking, the inmate trips, which sparks Sam's stress response in an already stressful situation.

Amygdala: OMG, the inmate is doing something unexpected. I'm in imminent danger. I think I'm going to die. [Cortisol surge.]

Hippocampus: [Crickets.]

PFC: [Clueless.]

Amygdala: I KNEW IT! IT'S AN EMERGENCY. LET'S DO THIS! FIGHT, PROTECT, RESTRAIN!

Mindfulness in Action: Sam's thinking brain comes back online, and he realizes he is choking the inmate. Because he has practiced mindfulness many times, his brain has built neural pathways that allow him to notice what is occurring and take appropriate action.

- Awareness: *Wow, I'm choking this guy out. How did I get here?*
- Paying attention: *Hmm, what are my thoughts right now? And what is my body telling me? Am I feeling any tension?*
- Present moment: *Okay, I feel a surge of fear, and I feel like I'm losing my temper. My face is hot and my neck is tense.*
- Non-judgmentally: *Yes, I lashed out (literally). But I am able to notice it now. Congrats to me for noticing what was happening!*

Mindfulness Intervention: *What intervention has worked for me in the past? I should take some deep breaths, with really long exhales.* [Cortisol level decreases by taking a breath.]

Amygdala: Hmmm, this might not be an emergency. What do you think, Hippocampus? Should we pass this possibly emergent information on?

Hippocampus: Sure, I will let the PFC know it might want to make some decisions.

PFC: Okay, I see what's going on. This guy just tripped—he wasn't assaulting us. Decrease neck pressure and slowly back off. Stay on guard, but it's okay to release him.

HOW MINDFULNESS HELPS

While the above breakdown probably seems like it would take a lot of time, it actually only takes a few seconds. It's like seeing a tree and just knowing it's a tree, rather than stopping to think, *That tall thing I see with green leaves and branches is a tree.* After seeing a tree so many times in your life, it's an automatic association. In the same way, repeated practice makes it almost automatic to bring awareness to your situation so that you can take deliberate and thoughtful action. Like any skill, the more you practice, the more it becomes second nature.

CONTEMPLATION QUESTIONS

Can you think of a time you had to perform while under stress? What happened?

____

____

____

____

____

DON'T FORGET!

Fill out the first column of the self-assessment chart before practicing the mindfulness intervention.

Mindfulness Intervention Self-Assessment

BREATHING

The self-assessment chart that follows is designed to track your progress. This chart will help you assess three things:

- How you feel before doing the mindfulness intervention, from 1 = you feel your best to 5 = you feel your worst
- How you feel after doing the mindfulness intervention, from 1 = you feel your best to 5 = you feel your worst
- How you felt while practicing the mindfulness intervention, from 1 = it was pleasant to 5 = it was unpleasant

Fill out the first column of the chart *before* you move on to the mindfulness intervention practice in this chapter. *After* you've practiced the intervention, fill out the second and third columns.

Remember that these assessments are subjective. There are no right or wrong answers and no judgment. And make it easy on yourself—write it down directly in the book, and you can always come back to it for reference.

MINDFULNESS INTERVENTION SELF-ASSESSMENT

Pre-assessment	Post-assessment	Summary Assessment
Overall Mood/Quality (1 = Best → 5 = Worst)	Overall Mood/Quality (1 = Best → 5 = Worst)	Quality of Intervention (1 = Pleasant → 5 = Unpleasant)

Mindfulness Intervention

BREATHING

This practice helps the brain learn to notice what is happening in the present moment without judgment. It can help you recognize all the different variables occurring in a situation and focus your attention where it's needed most.

How to Practice

Set a timer for practicing or do what feels comfortable for you.

1. **Find a seated position.** Sit in a way that is comfortable but not too relaxed. You should have a feeling of sitting upright but not "uptight." Allow your eyes to close or keep them open and focused on a single point.
2. **Notice your breath.** Bring your attention to how you are breathing. There is no right or wrong way to breathe, just breathe naturally. Notice as your belly or chest rises and falls, or how you feel the air come and go from your nostrils.
3. **Slow your breathing.** After a few breaths, begin to slow down your inhales and exhales. Focus on making your exhale longer than your inhale. To do this, try counting the length of your inhales. You can begin by making your inhale a three count and your exhale a seven count.
4. **Notice your thoughts.** As you breathe, you will notice that your mind will wander. Thoughts will come and go. You may even get caught up in a story, not realizing that you have been "thinking" until the end of the story.
5. **Refocus your attention on your breath.** When you catch your mind in a thought, notice it (*Thinking*) and guide your attention back to your breath. One of the goals of mindfulness is to simply notice. Every time you notice your mind has wandered, you are being mindful and are deep in the training. Try not to get caught up in judging or interpreting

your thoughts. Simply notice that you were thinking and return your attention to the breath.

6. **Three closing breaths.** Once you have practiced for a comfortable amount of time, take three deep closing breaths, exhaling longer than inhaling. Bring your attention to your feet on the ground and just think about what they feel like. Take one more breath and open your eyes, or just refocus on the room.

Mindfulness Intervention QR Code: Guided Breathing

You can check out a recorded guided practice here:

Mindfulness Intervention Self-Assessment

Return to the self-assessment chart to fill out the postassessment and summary assessment columns *after* you practice the mindfulness intervention.

CHAPTER 4

SCIENCE OF MINDFULNESS

"The eternal mystery of the world is its comprehensibility . . . The fact that it is comprehensible is a miracle."

– Albert Einstein

In this chapter, I will address:

- Tom's story of being consumed by road rage
- The science behind mindfulness
- What studies say about mindfulness
- Mindfulness intervention: **Listening**

ROAD RAGE—IT'S LEGIT!

Los Angeles, where I grew up, is known for its traffic, accidents, and gridlock. It can take over an hour to travel 15 miles on the freeway. And let me tell you, it's not an exaggeration when people say driving in L.A. is like playing *Frogger*, that ancient arcade game where you try to cross a street, weaving in and out of everything around you, without getting hit by a car.

While *Ms. Pac-Man* was more my father's jam when it came to video games, Tom Rollo did love a good real-life *Frogger* game. Every time we got in the car, he found a reason to drive as fast as he could, weaving in and out of traffic until he eventually lost his cool and became aggressive. It typically started with foul language under his breath, then progressed to yelling out the window, and eventually included his oh-so-Italian hand gestures, combined with honking his horn.

All of that was just phase 1. Phase 2 involved Tom driving extremely close to the other driver, whom he saw as the perpetrator of dangerous driving, while still performing the actions of phase 1. Phase 3 involved making a grandiose statement by purposefully cutting off said perpetrator, thereby weaponizing our car, and repeating phase 1 actions, this time on steroids: He would lean his entire body out the window (or roll down my passenger window and lean across me) while yelling.

Finally, if he felt he was not receiving an appropriate reaction, Tom resorted to phase 4. He would force the other driver to transition from driving to parking by chasing the perpetrator of dangerous driving off the freeway (or down the street), pull up next to them (really, *really* close), roll down the window (or worse, get out of the car), and give them a piece of his mind about how dangerously they were driving. (No need to point out the irony here.) Meanwhile, we kids nodded our heads in affirmation, infinitely proud of our dad for taking care of the world and keeping us safe.

IMPORTANT NOTE

I need to clarify something important here: Someone can be kind, empathetic, generous, loving, a community badass, and have some traits that aren't so great. This does not make them a bad person. It just means there's room for improvement—to fine-tune, recalibrate, make a few tactical adjustments. This book is not saying you suck if you blow up, fly off the handle, disassociate, or simply feel depressed, angry, or numb. You can be a good person and make mistakes. This book is about noticing what's occurring in your mind and adjusting your actions without judging yourself. It takes time. And it works.

LEARNED BEHAVIOR

We never really questioned our father's outbursts when we were young. It was our normal. We learned that strong reactions were appropriate behavior for a desired outcome. If you didn't like the way someone looked at you, you yelled; if you didn't like how they drove, you swerved toward them. I remember feeling energized when we would chase someone on the road, my excitement building and building until my dad exploded on someone, at which point my emotions peaked, and I would feel a wave of exhilaration rushing through me. My dad was protecting us, and justice had been served.

By the time I started driving, it felt natural to incorporate this approach into my driving. I didn't just repeat the traffic vigilantism that was modeled for me; I overtly sought it out, constantly scanning for annoying and irresponsible drivers so I could lash out and experience that rush I had felt as a kid. This was not a conscious choice; it just became part of my experience in a car. I never even considered there was any other way to drive.

Eventually, I realized this type of driving had a name: road rage. Doing research on concepts like emotional eruptions and anger management was the first time I examined my dad's road rage. The deeper I dove into the research on emotional dysregulation, uncontrolled outbursts, and emotional balance, the more I realized that his (and my) emotional outbursts were not isolated to driving but pervaded our approaches to life.

At a basic level, I knew that seeking out situations to create a heightened emotion was not a positive behavior, even though it secretly felt so good. This got me wondering: How *do* behaviors develop? Is the process the same for both good and bad traits? And most importantly, can we train our brains away from a negative behavior and toward a positive one?

FIRST RESPONDER MUSCLE MEMORY

Training the brain for a specific behavior is no different from training your body through working out. If you want to enhance a particular muscle, you isolate a muscle group and apply a focused exercise. For maximum results, you do that specific exercise a lot! The same goes for functional movement outcomes—that is, movements that have a specific purpose or goal. By repeating the same action over and over (and over), the muscles are not only building for that particular movement but the mind is also organizing around the muscles and movements recruited during this action and memorizing what to do when a stimulus for that movement shows up.

A great example of this process is learning how to shoot a basketball from the free throw line. The first time you walk up to the line, you're not quite sure how far apart to set your feet, if you should have straight legs or knees bent, how to hold and throw the ball, or even where to focus your gaze. The second time, you remember that last time you felt wobbly because your feet were too close together, and you instinctively make your stance wider this time. The time after that, you remember you need more bend in your knees, so you go a little deeper. Through trial and error, you begin to construct a series of movements that work for you. As you repeat that formula over and over, the actions become fine-tuned and even become second nature.

First Time: Feeling a Bit Stressed

- Where should I stand?
- How far apart should my feet be?
- How deep do I bend my knees?
- How do I hold the ball?
- How hard do I throw the ball?
- Where should I focus?

Repeat: A Little Less Stressed

- Go to spot
- Feet closer (my feet were too far apart last time)
- Deeper bend (legs felt stiff last time)
- Wide palm on ball
- Send it a bit harder
- Look at backboard

Repeat: Even Less Stressed

- Remember
- Adjust
- Remember
- Adjust
- Remember

Repeat: Can Now Focus on Fine Details

- Remember

- Fine-tune
- Remember
- Fine-tune
- Remember

First responders are required to undergo numerous trainings connected to very specific job-related tasks. A few examples:

Law Enforcement

- Task Action: Firing a weapon
- Outcome: Building muscle memory of position and accuracy

Fire Services

- Task Action: Connecting hose coupling to water source
- Outcome: Building agility and muscle recall while kneeling or holding hose to hip

Medical Services

- Task Action: Practicing chest compressions
- Outcome: Building muscle memory of movement and pressure efficiency

Dispatch

- Task Action: Assessing calls for directed operations and procedures
- Outcome: Building automatic response to dispatch appropriate resources (LE, FD, MED)

Corrections

- Task Action: Use of force and restraint techniques
- Outcome: Building muscle memory of level of force permitted

All these trainings are built on the premise that practicing an action trains both the brain and body to perform a task for a precise (or as close to precise as one can get) outcome. The more you practice, the more accurate you become. And the more accurate you become, the more efficient you become—that is, it takes much less thought to decide when and how to apply the action.

This ability of the brain to reorganize connections and strengthen the path between thinking of an action and taking that action is called **neuroplasticity**. Repeated actions trigger an actual change in the brain's structure—specifically, the creation of new neural pathways—which then feeds a physical and/or mental habit change. The larger number of neural pathways formed and reinforced by repetition, the stronger a habit becomes. These neural pathways can result in creating habits like biting nails or clicking a pen, or even bigger behaviors like habitual reactions to anger, anxiety, stress, and overwhelm.

Creating a behavior, whether it's positive or negative, is accomplished by repeating actions. So what actions can we take to shift our brains away from a bad behavior and toward a good behavior? And how do we make it stick?

There's a saying in the neuroscience world that goes, "Neurons that fire together, wire together." Essentially, neurons responding to the same stimulus link together, building even bigger bundles of connected information. The idea is that if you keep repeating a behavior, larger neuronal connections are created between all the thoughts and actions involved in that behavior, which makes the behavior increasingly easier to access—that is, it becomes instinctive or turns into a habit. Again, this is true for both positive and negative behaviors. Road rage is a great example of this. If a car cuts you off and you react aggressively toward the other driver, a neuron in your brain connects the incident of getting cut off with the emotion of anger. When it happens again, more neurons link up to reinforce this connection, which causes your fuse to get shorter. That is, the aggressive reaction requires less conscious choice or effort; it's becoming an instinct.

Habits and Neuroplasticity

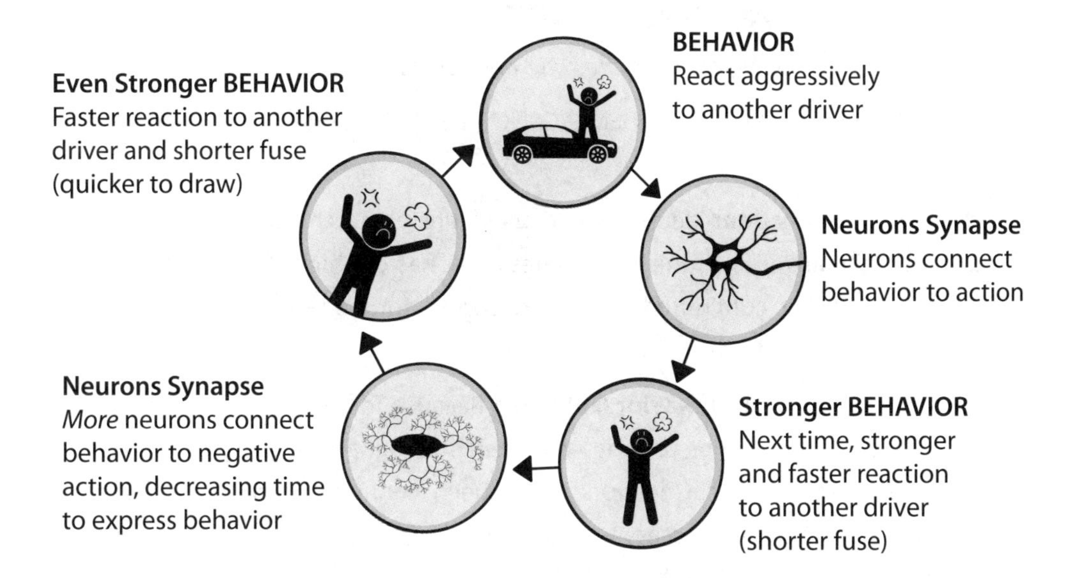

Another saying shows where mindfulness enters the picture: "Neurons that fall out of sync lose their link." When you stop performing a habitual action or interrupt it, the network of neuronal connections grows smaller, and it becomes more difficult to perform the action. If you've ever tried to learn a new language, you can easily relate to this. As soon as you stop using that second language, it becomes more difficult to recall the words and phrases you've learned. The same principle applies to negative behaviors and their outcomes. If you want to break a habit, you must practice interrupting the unwanted behavior and replacing it with the behavior you do want.

Practicing mindfulness can help accomplish this shift. Noticing a behavior you want to change gives you the opportunity to interrupt it when it shows up, and interruption decreases neuronal connections between the situational trigger and the behavior. Replacing it with a new behavior creates increased neuron activity that builds a new connection to that situational trigger. In this way, you can train your brain away from aggressive driving and toward, for example, square breathing; away from yelling at your child and toward taking a walk; away from mindless eating for self-soothing and toward mindfully eating for health. The more you repeat these positive behaviors, the stronger they become.

TACTICAL BRAIN TRAINING IN ACTION

Scenario: Tom is driving on a busy freeway, and someone cuts him off.

Amygdala: I KNEW IT! IT'S AN EMERGENCY. LET'S DO THIS! FIGHT, PROTECT, RESTRAIN!

Neuronal Connection: Neurons send messages along the path created by that stimulus (i.e., all the other times a car has cut him off) and connect to previously configured neuron networks for behavior outcome (an aggressive reaction).

Neurons Synapse for Behavior Outcome: Because Tom has experienced this situation many times and has repeated this behavioral outcome many times, large neuronal networks have been configured. These networks allow for immediate access to reactions, causing him to instantly lose his cool. He automatically honks his horn, pulls the car really close to other cars, yells, throws out hand gestures.

Mindfulness in Action:

- Awareness: *Wow, I just yelled at someone for getting too close to me.*
- Paying attention: *What are my thoughts right now? And what is my body telling me? Am I feeling any tension?*
- Present moment: *Okay, I am gripping the steering wheel, and I feel like my eyes are bulging out of my head.*
- Non-judgmentally: *Yup, I almost hit that car on purpose and cursed someone out, all with my kids in the back seat.* And *I was able to notice it. Congrats to me for noticing what was happening!*

Mindfulness Intervention: *What can I do right now to calm myself down? Maybe I can try a* ***Listening*** *intervention for a few minutes. I can focus on sounds in the car, or I can play music and pay attention to a particular instrument or the sounds of someone singing.*

Neuronal Connection: By redirecting away from the previous habitual aggressive reaction and toward a calming action, new neurons are linked and new connections begin to build.

Neurons Synapse for Behavior Outcome: The same stimulus occurs (being cut off by someone), but the newly formed networks become connected to a new outcome (**Listening** intervention, which calms and decreases stress).

The more times you redirect your feelings of overreaction toward the application of a mindfulness intervention, the stronger that new connection becomes. The brain is tactically rewiring for a new outcome while dissolving the wiring for the old outcome.

Action/behavior creates neural pathways

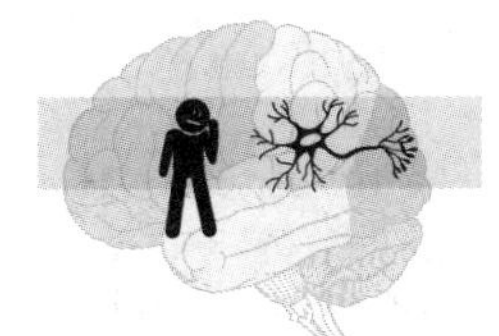

Repeated action/behavior strengthens pathway, creating a habit

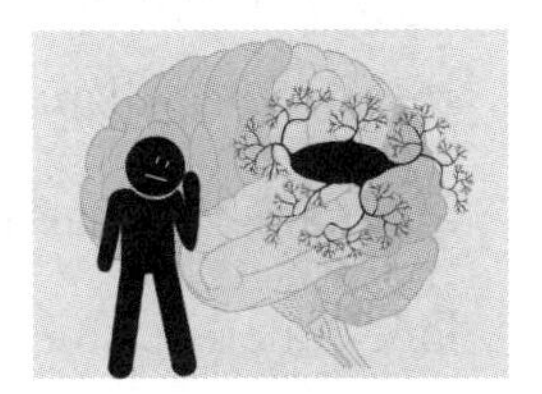

Decrease in action/behavior weakens habit

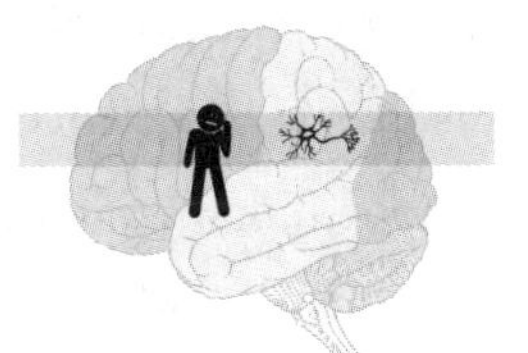

DON'T JUDGE, JUST OBSERVE

So yes, habits are created by repeating the same responses to experiences. This then prompts the question: Is it in our control to influence/change these habits? It's crazy to think we can actually generate structural changes in our brains just by choosing which actions to repeat. But it's true! In fact, a study that looked at the brain using an MRI showed deeper and wider grooves—new neuronal pathways—in the regions of the brain concerned with cardiorespiratory control related to taking a specific action, like focused breathing. The findings of this study showed that these pathways could account for positive cognitive and parasympathetic outcomes such as a state of relaxation, slower heart rate, reduced blood pressure, and improved recovery and thinking, all of which play an important role in stress reduction.*

For first responders, who are under immense pressure to not only perform but to perform accurately, training the brain to self-regulate under stress can have a positive impact on many outcomes:

- Maintain composure and think clearly while interacting with erratic individuals
- Generate a sense of calm during volatile traffic stop interactions
- Increase awareness of surroundings in a safety-compromised environment (such as standing on a burning roof or entering a structure where there are armed assailants)
- Maintain clear communication with a 911 caller and team members
- Fine-tune assessment skills during a traumatic event or diagnosis

Regardless of the situation (stress, emergency, surprise) or the magnitude of any emotion that is experienced, mindfulness trains the brain to accept the present moment without judgment. Judgment adds a layer of stress that inhibits our ability to regulate ourselves and respond reasonably to a situation and the emotions it brings up. Rather than letting the mind spin down a rabbit hole of perceived issues or emotions, we can experience situations in their raw and unprocessed forms without attaching to them. In other words, we're training for the ability to witness an emotion, acknowledge that it's there, then decide what to do about it.

Think of it as watching a movie. As an observer, you see what is happening and maybe even feel emotions about it, but you are not *in* the movie, experiencing the situation or interacting with characters themselves. As a result, you're much better at predicting what the outcome of a situation or interaction will be—you might not know what's waiting at the bottom of the dark stairs in the old house, but you definitely know that the person in the horror movie shouldn't be walking down there.

Similarly, training to observe your emotions, rather than interact with them, allows you to perceive events in a new way. The result is an ability to comprehend a situation and to be aware of any emotion it brings up without needing to engage with it.

---

* Vestergaard-Poulsen, P., van Beek, M., Skewes, J., Bjarkam, C. R., Stubberup, M., Bertelsen, J., & Roepstorff, A. (2009). Long-term meditation is associated with increased gray matter density in the brain stem. *NeuroReport, 20*(2), 170–174. https://doi.org/10.1097/WNR.0b013e328320012a

When you can essentially sit back and watch the emotions that are arising within you, you create space to incorporate a mindfulness intervention, which leads to regulation of your nervous system, which then empowers you to respond rather than react. By creating space between an emotion and how we interact with it, we not only strengthen our ability to respond with awareness, purpose, and control but also reinforce the desire to decrease the old habitual reaction (losing control or detaching from the situation) and increase our ability to respond mindfully.

PRACTICING MINDFULNESS

Practicing mindfulness through awareness and tactical interventions trains the mind to observe what's occurring without attaching to it. By doing this over and over, the brain undergoes structural changes that make it easier to maintain emotional balance and access the response you really want to offer. This also leads to a physical response, such as decreased blood pressure. Incorporating a mindfulness intervention in the moment of stress helps increase awareness, clarity, and intention, which allows us to better manage emotions like anger, anxiety, stress, and disassociation.

CONTEMPLATION QUESTIONS

Can you think of an example when you reacted without thinking while working? Maybe a time when you looked back and thought, *That was a really big reaction for a minor situation*. What happened?

____

____

____

Now think of a time when you really wanted to lose it, but you were able to control it and respond instead of react. What occurred?

____

____

____

DON'T FORGET!

Fill out the first column of the self-assessment chart before practicing the mindfulness intervention.

Mindfulness Intervention Self-Assessment

LISTENING

The self-assessment chart that follows is designed to track your progress. This chart will help you assess three things:

- How you feel before doing the mindfulness intervention, from 1 = you feel your best to 5 = you feel your worst
- How you feel after doing the mindfulness intervention, from 1 = you feel your best to 5 = you feel your worst
- How you felt while practicing the mindfulness intervention, from 1 = it was pleasant to 5 = it was unpleasant

Fill out the first column of the chart *before* you move on to the mindfulness intervention practice in this chapter. *After* you've practiced the intervention, fill out the second and third columns.

Remember that these assessments are subjective. There are no right or wrong answers and no judgment. And make it easy on yourself—write it down directly in the book, and you can always come back to it for reference.

MINDFULNESS INTERVENTION SELF-ASSESSMENT

Pre-assessment	Post-assessment	Summary Assessment
Overall Mood/Quality (1 = Best → 5 = Worst)	Overall Mood/Quality (1 = Best → 5 = Worst)	Quality of Intervention (1 = Pleasant → 5 = Unpleasant)

Mindfulness Intervention

LISTENING

This practice is good for honing and focusing your attention. It can help bring awareness to your surroundings, both internal and external. It also trains you to create a sense of calm by directing your attention away from a stressful thought or feeling, allowing you to focus on something innocuous, such as a sound.

How to Practice

Set a timer for practicing or do what feels comfortable for you.

1. **Find a seated position.** Sit in a way that is comfortable but not too relaxed. You should have a feeling of sitting upright but not "uptight." Allow your eyes to close or keep them open and focused on a single point.
2. **Notice what you hear.** Be still, allow your hearing to be sensitive, and listen to sounds as they occur. During moments of silence, notice the quality of the silence. Is it loud, soft, continuous, pleasant, bothersome? Sounds will come and go; no need to seek them out. Listen.
3. **Notice the mind.** When you do hear a sound, you will most likely name it (e.g., *Door opening*, *Dog barking*, *Person walking*). Notice that you named it, then move on, redirecting your attention back to listening once again.
4. **Release judgment.** Allow yourself to notice the sounds without attached judgment. When you do notice judgments arise, refocus your mind on listening again. For example, when you realize you are having thoughts—like *Why do I keep losing my focus?* or *Why can't I just notice it as "sound" without having an internal conversation about it?*—shift your awareness and begin to listen again.
5. **Three closing breaths.** Once you have practiced for a comfortable amount of time, take three deep closing breaths, exhaling longer than

inhaling. Bring your attention to your feet on the ground and think about what they feel like. Take one more breath and open your eyes, or just refocus on the room.

Mindfulness Intervention QR Code: Guided Listening

You can check out a recorded guided practice here:

Mindfulness Intervention Self-Assessment

Return to the self-assessment chart to fill out the postassessment and summary assessment columns *after* you practice the mindfulness intervention.

CHAPTER 5

RESPONDING VERSUS REACTING

"There is simply no easy way to hold infinite space in a finite brain."

– Katie Mack

In this chapter, I will address:

- Jill's story of reacting negatively when under stress
- The difference between responding and reacting
- How mindfulness helps us move toward actively responding
- Mindfulness intervention: **Square Breathing**

BEYOND A TOLERABLE THRESHOLD

Jill had been a firefighter and paramedic for over six years, working night shifts in a particularly violent neighborhood, which meant nonstop action. More often than not, she would stay out all night on back-to-back calls. The schedule, though grueling, was great in that it allowed her to be a part of her kids' lives during the day. After working all night long, Jill would arrive home just in time to make her kids breakfast and help them get ready for school. She would drive them to school, run any necessary errands while she was out, take care of a few household things, then go to sleep. The morning tended to be a bit hectic, as she was typically still amped up from working the previous night but also physically and mentally exhausted. She explained to me that she was noticing that it was getting harder and harder for her to control her irritation toward everyone: her kids, her coworkers, her neighbors, even her partner. She was seeing a connection between being stressed and having a short fuse.

One particular night, Jill was called to a shooting, which was not uncommon. This time, however, it was an adolescent who had been shot, on purpose, by his mother. For a mother like Jill, the situation brought up a lot of hard emotions. The emotional damage was only compounded when she was not able to save the boy's life.

By the time she was driving her son to school the next morning, Jill was well beyond her emotional threshold, overcome with all the pain surrounding loss of life, loss of a son, abuse, societal failures, and her self-perceived inability to do more to help the injured child survive. While she was driving, her son was sitting in the front passenger seat, looking down on his phone—listening to music, looking at TikTok, communicating on Snapchat, and probably 20 other things. After the harrowing tragedy she'd witnessed the night before, Jill wanted nothing more than to connect with her son. She started with some small talk but got little response. Hoping a pointed question might get a longer response, she decided to ask something specific about how he was doing on an upcoming school project. She asked him the same question not once, not twice, but three times. Still no real response. On her fourth try, which was much louder and very irritated, her son finally looked up. His face showed complete and utter contempt, and his response was filled with annoyance.

At that point, Jill hit her limit. In a split second, she pulled the car over on the side of a very busy road, got out and walked to the other side, abruptly dragged her son out of the front seat, pushed him up against the car, and began yelling at him. Thrust outside her window of tolerance, Jill was no longer thinking; she was simply reacting on frustration and pure adrenaline.

I relate to her story on so many levels. As a kid, I personally experienced many situations like this. I can remember getting annoyed with my dad over something small, like not understanding a math problem he was explaining, and responding in a bitchy, irreverent teen tone, only to meet the same outcome as Jill's son: my father exploding like we were in a war zone and I was an insubordinate grunt. But I also relate to this story from Jill's perspective. Even as I am writing, I can viscerally feel the frustration caused by my own teenage daughters speaking to me in an irreverent, dismissive tone, and I can name over 20 times when I reacted by screaming at the top of my lungs, as if we were all under attack. In those moments, it felt like the only way to deal with the perceived emergency was to flip my lid.

FLIPPING YOUR LID

"Flipping your lid" is a helpful phrase used to explain how the brain becomes emotional rather than rational when under stress. Dr. Daniel Siegel (the same one who coined the "window of tolerance") puts this phrase in the context of emotional regulation. In his book *Mindsight*, he explains that in an emergency, real or perceived, the thinking part of the brain (i.e., the PFC; see diagram in chapter 3) goes offline.* This essentially translates to a disconnect between the thinking brain and the emotional brain. Imagine your brain as a closed fist, working smoothly when all is well, the various parts in close communication with each other. Now, open your hand. This is what happens when you're stressed; it feels like the parts of your brain are disconnected.

The Hand Model of the Brain

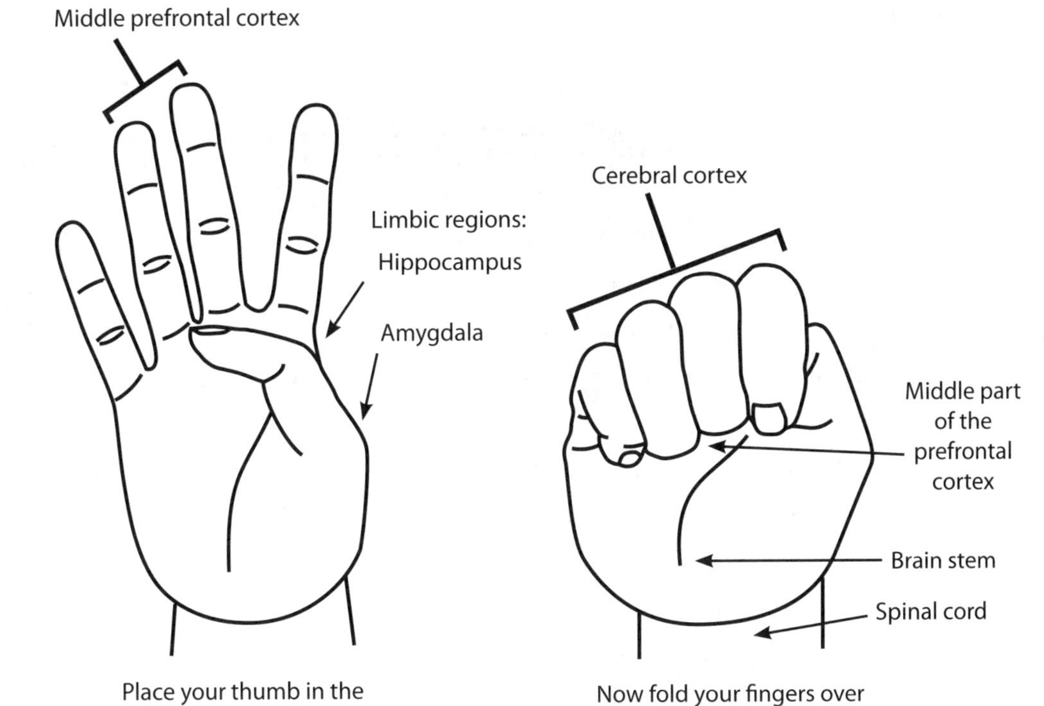

Adapted from *Mindsight* (p. 15) by D. J. Siegel, 2010, Bantam. Copyright © 2010 by Mind Your Brain, Inc.

* Siegel, D. J. (2010). *Mindsight: The new science of personal transformation*. Bantam Books.

As we learned in the last chapter, the PFC is responsible for executive functioning—problem-solving, reasoning, self-reflection, impulse control—which keeps a "lid" on the rest of the emotional brain's simmering activity. So it makes sense that when the PFC goes offline, the "pot" is liable to boil over and you "flip your lid."

Since one of the amygdala's primary jobs is to react to a threat, it makes sense that it's programmed to be the boss during a stressful situation. This system can be a great protective reaction in times of real danger. For example, if you're out for a walk and a speeding car comes down the street, your amygdala will show up with an airhorn and a megaphone: YOU'RE GOING TO GET HIT! JUMP OUT OF THE WAY!

However, sometimes the boss can be wrong. In Jill's situation, her preexisting state of high stress caused her to interpret her son's disrespect as an emergency. At that point, the brain was no longer an integrated unit, just separated parts reacting (or not reacting) on their own. The amygdala turned up the heat, the stressful emotions in her brain boiled over, and the PFC lid flipped, causing her to react from a state of fight—no thinking, just acting.

TRAINING FOR RESPONSE

Interestingly, research suggests that we can bring the PFC back online with a very simple action: taking a breath. A study published in *NeuroImage* suggests that during emotional stimulation, slow, purposeful breathing can downregulate the activation in the amygdala, allowing the PFC to reintegrate with the rest of the brain. In other words, focused breathing can calm the amygdala, resulting in a decrease of our heightened emotions, which reestablishes connection with our executive functioning and reenables our powers of thinking, processing, and reasoning.*

The difficult part, of course, is knowing when to take that slow, purposeful breath. Fortunately, TBT teaches us to identify this important juncture. Training for awareness helps you notice when you have moved outside your window of tolerance and are in a heightened emotional state. Training to incorporate a mindfulness intervention then helps you downregulate so you can bring your PFC back online.

Another way of saying it is that TBT tips the scales from a **reactive state** to a **responsive state**. A responsive state comes from using an integrated brain that

---

* Doll, A., Hölzel, B. K., Bratec, S. M., Boucard, C. C., Xie, X., Wohlschläger, A. M., & Sorg, C. (2016). Mindful attention to breath regulates emotions via increased amygdala–prefrontal cortex connectivity. *NeuroImage, 134*, 305–313. https://doi.org/10.1016/j.neuroimage.2016.03.041

empowers us with control over our actions, so that we can decide how to act based on gathered information and analytical thinking, rather than a rush of emotion. This is not to say that every decision will have the great outcome you're aiming for. It just means that you are using clear thought and agency in choosing what action to take. Practicing mindfulness means training to notice what frustration (or irritation, or sadness, or distraction) feels like, what it does to your mind and body in the moment, as you hit an edge of what is tolerable. In short, mindfulness trains the brain to change its relationship with stimuli.

> *Going over the edge is normal. It happens to all of us. For the purposes of TBT, the fact of it happening is less important than the realization that it has happened. TBT is about noticing what's occurring for us and being intentional about what we do next.*

If you think about it, stimulus can be anything. A noise, a bad driver, an annoying child, or even a rainy day. Since those things are never going away, the idea is to retrain the brain to relate to the stimulus in a more productive way. Maybe on a rainy day (stimulus) you immediately react with doom and gloom: *Crap, another rainy day.* This is a great time to practice TBT. First, you notice that you feel sad, restless, or disappointed that your plans will have to be postponed. Next, you reflect on your reaction: *Hmm, this is making me feel* ____. Then, you choose a response that changes the situation—perhaps you choose to think about what you can accomplish on a rainy day, like working on a project you never seem to have time to do. This changes the equation from reactive (annoyed without thinking about it) to responsive (controlling the situation by coming up with a plan of action).

At a higher level of stress, maybe something occurs in the environment (or even within your own mind) that pushes you to your limit. This stress signals the amygdala to go into emergency mode, which leads to primal reactions like anger, exploding, disconnecting, running—reactions that, in most cases, don't serve you or those around you. Here again, TBT helps you notice you have hit an edge (or notice that you have gone over the edge), then apply a mindfulness intervention to bring you back from the edge and into a rational state of mind so that the next action you take is one that you can feel good about.

TACTICAL BRAIN TRAINING IN ACTION

Scenario: After a traumatic night at work, Jill is exhausted, yet she must now get her son ready and drive him to school.

Window of Tolerance: With her tolerance already down, Jill is pushing through, but with every added negative stimulus, she gets closer and closer to the edge. The final straw is her interaction (or lack thereof) with her son. This sends her beyond what is tolerable.

Amygdala: He's not responding. We need him to listen! This is an emergency—we will not survive if he doesn't listen!

PFC: [Disconnected, hears nothing but background noise.]

Amygdala: Pull the car over, and get in his face. He will have to listen if we are in his face! We are running out of time—DO IT NOW!

Mindfulness in Action:

- Awareness: *Wow, his face looks terrified and confused. I'm guessing I went over the edge.*
- Paying attention: *Hm. What are my thoughts right now? What is my body doing?*
- Present moment: *I'm standing on the side of a busy road and I am holding my son's collar while pushing him against the car.*
- Non-judgmentally: *Okay, this happened. I am glad I realized when I did. Great job noticing!*

PFC: It's time to take some breaths and allow the nervous system to regulate and balance. We need to get off this busy road, get back in the car, and begin again. It's time for a mindfulness intervention. Which one will work right now?

Mindfulness Intervention: *Square Breathing*—*I can do it while standing here; I don't need to close my eyes or sit down.*

Amygdala: Well, I guess this wasn't really an emergency. It's annoying, but not urgent. I think all is okay. Let's get back into the window of tolerance.

RECONNECTING WITH MINDFULNESS

Maybe during a chaotic moment, you say to yourself, *Uh-oh, I'm about to flip my lid.* Because of your repeated practice, you remember it's time to downregulate emotions and respond versus react. But what if during this chaotic time, the situation does not allow for you to sit comfortably, relax your body, and focus on a deep breathing intervention?

Mindfulness comes in many forms. Some interventions are more detailed and take more time. Others are quick and easy to practice anywhere, anytime. Experience and practice help us assess our needs, consider the environment, and choose a mindfulness intervention that works best for our given situation.

Square Breathing is great for moments when a simpler approach is better. This mindfulness intervention can be practiced while on duty, walking to a vehicle, traveling to or from a crime scene, in between calls, in line at the grocery store, while making dinner, in the shower, and even while in the middle of high reactivity, such as during an argument. Square breathing helps regulate the nervous system by slowing down the breath while also redirecting thoughts away from the chaos. It's like taking a cognitive "step" away from the stressful or traumatic situation so that your brain can regroup and process more effectively. After a few loops around the square, the mind and body settle, allowing for more thoughtful and focused decision-making, versus hasty and emotionally based decision-making. Square breathing sharpens your in-the-moment awareness, helping you make more conscious choices that are better aligned with how you want to show up in the world and in relation to others.

CONTEMPLATION QUESTIONS

Practicing mindfulness interventions redirects neuronal activity away from an impulsive reaction and toward a thought-out response. Think of an on-duty incident that triggered an emotional response in you. What happened?

____

____

____

____

What was your reaction?

____

____

____

____

How could you change that reaction to a thought-out response?

____

____

____

____

DON'T FORGET!

Fill out the first column of the self-assessment chart before practicing the mindfulness intervention.

Mindfulness Intervention Self-Assessment

SQUARE BREATHING

The self-assessment chart that follows is designed to track your progress. This chart will help you assess three things:

- How you feel before doing the mindfulness intervention, from 1 = you feel your best to 5 = you feel your worst
- How you feel after doing the mindfulness intervention, from 1 = you feel your best to 5 = you feel your worst
- How you felt while practicing the mindfulness intervention, from 1 = it was pleasant to 5 = it was unpleasant

Fill out the first column of the chart *before* you move on to the mindfulness intervention practice in this chapter. *After* you've practiced the intervention, fill out the second and third columns.

Remember that these assessments are subjective. There are no right or wrong answers and no judgment. And make it easy on yourself—write it down directly in the book, and you can always come back to it for reference.

MINDFULNESS INTERVENTION SELF-ASSESSMENT

Pre-assessment	Post-assessment	Summary Assessment
Overall Mood/Quality (1 = Best → 5 = Worst)	Overall Mood/Quality (1 = Best → 5 = Worst)	Quality of Intervention (1 = Pleasant → 5 = Unpleasant)

Mindfulness Intervention

SQUARE BREATHING

This practice is good for specific and focused attention, allowing for a controlled breathing pattern with defined parameters. It can be implemented during high-stress situations, without having to step away or even close your eyes, allowing the nervous system to regulate during a moment of chaos.

How to Practice

Set a timer for practicing or do what feels comfortable for you.

1. **Begin by choosing a posture that is comfortable for you.** Either sit in a way that is comfortable or stand against a wall. You should have a feeling of sitting or standing tall, in a way that creates a sense of being aware of your surroundings. Allow your eyes to close or keep them open and focused on a single point in front of you.
2. **Imagine the shape of a square.** Imagine a square, four sides, all equal in length. Either take your finger and trace the square, or use your mind to simply imagine traveling around the square.
3. **Inhale and exhale.** Connect your breath to the movement around the square:
    a. *Inhale—Lower Left Side:* Beginning on the lower left side, inhale as you imagine following the movement up the left side of the square. You can use a specified count (e.g., four seconds), or go at a pace that is comfortable.
    b. *Hold—Top of Square:* Now hold your breath as you imagine traversing across the top of the square.
    c. *Exhale—Upper Right Side:* Exhale as you follow the right side of the square down to the bottom. You can use a specified count (e.g., four seconds), or go at a pace that is comfortable.

d. *Hold—Bottom of Square:* Again, hold your breath as you traverse across the bottom from right to left.

e. *Repeat:* Inhale, hold, exhale, hold.

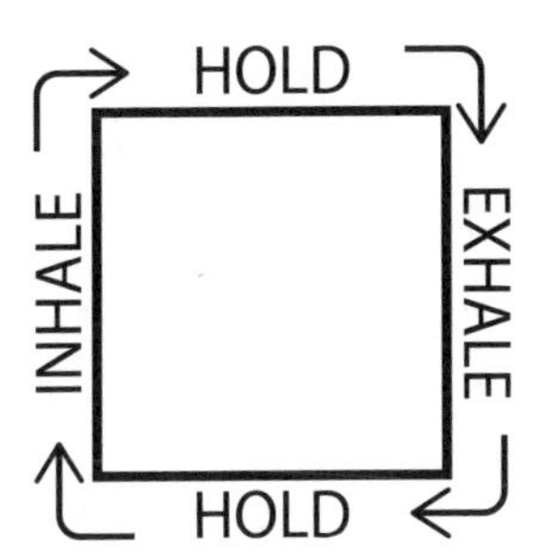

4. **Focus and visualization.** As you visualize the square, continue to synchronize your breath, creating a sense of balance and control. As you breathe, try to feel more stable and focused with each rotation around the square.
5. **Closing square.** Decide on your final square and, when completed, open your eyes or refocus on the room.

Mindfulness Intervention QR Code: Guided Square Breathing

You can check out a recorded guided practice here:

Mindfulness Intervention Self-Assessment

Return to the self-assessment chart to fill out the postassessment and summary assessment columns *after* you practice the mindfulness intervention.

CHAPTER 6

NOTICING TRIGGERS
(ACTIVATION VERSUS DEACTIVATION)

"We are made of star-stuff. We are a way
for the universe to know itself."

– *Carl Sagan*

In this chapter, I will address:

- George's story of an unexpected off-duty encounter
- Identifying triggers
- How mindfulness helps identify external and internal triggers
- Mindfulness intervention: **Signals**

SUDDEN CHANGE

George is not a small guy; most people would say that he looks really intimidating. He's tall and muscular, with a shaved head and tattoos everywhere. When on duty, he is a force to be reckoned with. (Meanwhile, when off duty, he is more like a giant teddy bear.) George works the gang unit and has spent over 10 years undercover. He loves his job, even though it sometimes causes strife in his life. Over the years of my conducting trainings at his agency, George and I built a relationship surrounding the need for officer wellness. I came to rely on him for brainstorming ideas about how we could improve stress management within his field.

One day, we were heading to lunch together, talking about some upcoming mindfulness trainings, when things got a little weird. As we walked into the restaurant, the teddy bear I was used to working with suddenly became highly agitated and started to act aggressive. We pushed through the tension, but lunch was not very enjoyable for either of us. I asked him what was up, and he said, "I'm just in a bad mood. No reason."

As we left the restaurant and began walking back to the parking lot, I noticed George do a double take to our left. When I looked over, I saw a group of men hanging out beside a short wall, near another restaurant. "Look down," George said to me, "and pick it up; we gotta get out of here now." It reminded me of when my dad would say "duck" and I would just duck, no questions asked. I had the same reaction on this day—I didn't pause, I didn't look around, I just booked it out of there. We got in our respective cars and went our separate ways. I figured I would ask him about it later, when we were away from what I now surmised was possible danger.

When I asked George about that situation later in the week, he explained that one of the guys we saw as we left the restaurant was an active gang member with whom George had recently had a confrontation. He did not want the guy to see him, and he *really* didn't want the guy to associate me with him. What I'd initially interpreted as aggression during lunch was, in fact, his unprocessed awareness regarding the possible danger we were in.

UNIDENTIFIED TRIGGER

George's reaction made sense to me, but I wanted to know more about how he had experienced it. When we did a mental walk-through of our entire lunch meeting, he said he had felt something was not quite right the second we walked into the restaurant. He recalled immediately feeling like he was "in a bad mood" and just wanted to leave from the minute we sat down to eat. We decided to do a retroactive step-by-step analysis of our meeting:

- Arrived at the same time (all good)
- Parked next to one another (good)

- Got out of our cars (still good)
- Left the parking lot together (still going strong)
- Walked toward the restaurant (what could go wrong?)
- Walked into the restaurant (*screech!*—mood shift)

As we replayed our approach to the restaurant entrance, George had an *aha!* moment. He recalled that as he reached for the door, his peripheral vision caught the group of guys leaning against the wall. No biggie, right? It's not uncommon for people to hang out in groups. Moreover, we were nowhere near the neighborhoods he worked, so there was presumably no reason for George to be on the lookout for an adversary—why, then, would he be overly concerned? But here's the interesting part. When he initially saw these guys, it was so out of context that his conscious mind simply skipped over the image, but his subconscious mind still caught it and set off his "spidey sense." And because he was not consciously aware of what was occurring, he didn't know how to identify what he was feeling, so he simply labeled it as "a bad mood." To use the metaphor we learned in the previous chapter, George's "lid" had been knocked askew, and thus his thoughts were not completely integrated, which made it difficult for him to notice what was simmering in his mind and deactivate it.

Anytime something occurs in our environment—an action, a conversation, even the sight of something static—the mind and body register what is occurring, regardless of our conscious awareness. If the occurrence is triggering for us, the body can experience a strong emotional reaction and even physical sensations. Triggers can be mental (internal) or environmental (external) and can occur from input received from any of our senses: sight, sound, touch, smell, taste. The resulting effects can include feelings of agitation, overwhelm, fear, stress, and even numbness. Experiencing a trigger can also cause distraction, ruminating thoughts, flashbacks, and difficulties with concentration.

It's important to note that none of the feelings or sensations related to being triggered are wrong, in and of themselves. Avoidance, fear, anger, and silence are all very safe strategies your body has developed to protect you. Noticing the feelings is the important part, as they are indications that something is occurring (internally or externally), and it is somehow affecting you. Instead of judging the feeling (or yourself for having it), simply recognize it for what it is: a needed nudge to take an action.

> *It's important to know that triggers are normal. Everyone has them, and they come in many forms. In fact, they can be beneficially informative. The key is to notice and manage those triggers, using these four steps:*
>
> 1. *Become aware of being triggered*
> 2. *Don't judge yourself for having a trigger*
> 3. *Be curious about what led to the trigger*
> 4. *Take an action to help manage your response to the trigger*

DETECTING ACTIVATION

There is a growing body of research investigating ways to improve **interoceptive processing**—that is, our ability to detect sensations arising within the body. This ability is important because when we can tune into the physical sensation of an emotion, we can use that sensory information to help regulate the emotion while it is occurring. It might not sound like much, but it can make a huge difference in our quality of life.

For instance, what if you could feel anger in a physical form? Maybe every time you get angry, you clench your fists or start to clamp down on your jaw. If you were able to notice this while it was happening, you could use that physical information to create curiosity about the situation. If you feel your jaw tighten, you can think, *What's happening that is making me tighten my jaw?*

The interesting part about this process is that even just asking that question helps decrease your stress level by creating some space between the trigger and the emotion. That space helps your cortisol levels decrease, which then empowers you to respond versus react.

Still, being able to tap into a sensation can be challenging. Let's give it quick try. Think about your kneecap—can you feel it just by thinking about it? What about your hand—can you mentally "feel" your hand? That one might be easier, as we are used to touching things with our hands. How about your shins? Can you feel those in your mind?

Some bodily sensations are obvious and don't need a lot of training to notice. For example, you know that a feeling of emptiness in your stomach is connected to hunger, and a feeling of heavy eyes or limbs is connected to fatigue. In these cases, connecting a sensation with an appropriate action or emotion is clear (you need to eat or sleep). But there are many instances where the connection is not obvious. Like George, you may suddenly find yourself feeling edgy: your shoulders tight, your hands clenched, your jaw clamped down, or your mood simply gone bad . . . and you have no idea why. But there's always a reason someone ends up in a bad mood. Something has occurred in the environment, either outside you or inside, that has triggered you.

Interoception basically means gathering the sensory input we receive all day long, so that we can name it and connect the bodily sensation with a thought, and vice versa. Interoception is important for understanding how our body interprets and reacts to things like sadness, fatigue, fear, and hunger. It plays a key role in emotional regulation and helps us understand emotional reactions and emotional needs.

Guess what helps connect the dots between a body sensation and mind? That's right—mindfulness. Mindfulness interventions train the brain to notice that a change has developed in the body and recognize it as a signal that a mental shift has occurred. Our body holds a ton of information that can help us act with clear purpose and efficiency. The trick is to learn how to listen to the information and identify the shifts as they are happening. TBT helps you learn to identify when you are moving into things like discomfort, agitation, avoidance, and fear. You are training yourself to think of these signals as warning signs that you have been activated and are outside your window of tolerance. These warning signs can show up as a mood shift, spiraling thoughts, feelings like sadness or overwhelm, images running through the mind, or tension in the body.

Warning Signs That You Are Outside Your Window of Tolerance

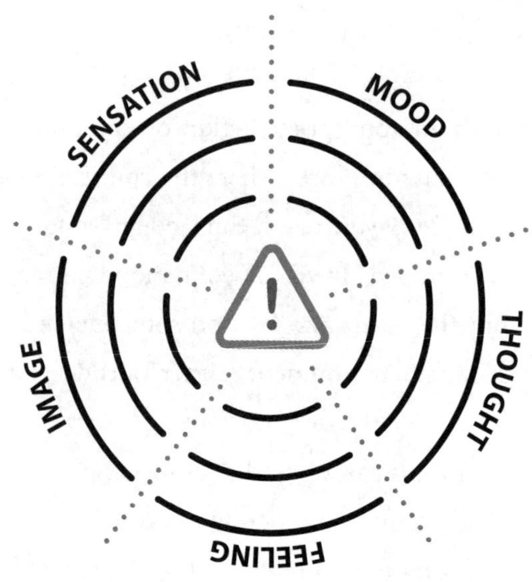

Mindfulness interventions like **Signals** (at the end of this chapter) and **Body Scan** (at the end of chapter 15) help us increase awareness of these warning signs. Through repeated training, you begin to identify a physical sensation that you can then associate with an emotion or thought, then connect the two with a situationally appropriate action. Mindfulness trains the brain to be curious and ask questions like:

- *I'm clenching my teeth; I wonder what's going on?*
- *Wow, I had to get out of there fast. What just triggered me?*
- *Why do I suddenly feel like I can't breathe? Am I being triggered right now?*

This type of awareness can take you from an activated state and move you to a deactivated state, regardless of when the awareness occurred. Once you can notice sensations, you are one step closer to taking meaningful and conscious actions that serve your well-being and that of the people around you.

CHANGING THE NARRATIVE

It's true that experiencing a trigger can cause distraction, ruminating thoughts, flashbacks, and difficulties with concentration. Still, becoming triggered does not have to be negative. With proper training, the brain begins to think of triggers as data—that is, information from the external and/or internal environment that can be useful when acknowledged and properly assessed. TBT helps us manage a triggered emotional state by realizing it is happening, being curious about why it is happening, then applying a mindfulness intervention that helps us cope.

Along with changing the narrative from "being triggered is bad" to "triggering is just information," you can also shift from thoughts like *If only I responded earlier* or *If only I didn't react the way I reacted* to more accepting thoughts. This can look like *Great job noticing when I did* or *Wow, I noticed I lashed out at someone, but I was then able to assess and realize something had happened that put me in a bad mood.* The change in perspective helps us acknowledge that it's never too late to change course, that there is always time to begin again. And again. And again.

TACTICAL BRAIN TRAINING IN ACTION

Scenario: George is unconsciously triggered, which leads to an unconscious change in his demeanor.

Window of Tolerance: George hits an edge and is not sure how to interact. He reverts to a familiar hypervigilant state, which looks like anger and frustration.

Internal Signal: A cue is received from the environment (he sees the bad guys) that his brain tags as *danger.*

Amygdala: Hey! I'm not sure what I just saw, but I'm pretty sure we are in danger. I suggest we get ready for a fight.

PFC: [Always a little clueless in these moments.] Keep walking through the door. We are supposed to be having lunch right now.

Mindfulness in Action:

- Awareness: *Wow, everything was fine one minute, and now I suddenly feel a negative shift in my mood.*
- Paying attention: *I should figure out what's going on or what happened.*
- Present moment: *My heart is beating fast and I feel agitated, like something bad is about to happen.*
- Non-judgmentally: *Apparently something triggered my sense of threat. Glad I caught it now, though. I'll deactivate the trigger while staying aware.*

Mindfulness Intervention: *Maybe if I connect to a body sensation, I can figure out when the mood shift occurred.*

PFC: Now that I can think clearly, let's remain calm while we create an exit strategy to avoid the possible danger.

PRACTICING MINDFULNESS

Mindfulness teaches us that our thoughts constantly come and go. Sometimes we know what we are thinking, and sometimes we are not connected to our thoughts at all. By training ourselves to pay attention, we are creating a link between unconsciousness and consciousness.

Triggers oftentimes land in the unconscious bucket. Data is collected and stored but never really sorted through. As bigger data items collect, like strong emotions, they spill over into the conscious areas of the mind and can show up as a mood shift or a sensation in the body, like a headache or neck pain. For example, a firefighter I worked with suddenly found he had a strong dislike for grocery stores. He explained that every time he walked into a grocery store, he would suddenly change his mind and walk out. Working through this backward (as I did with George), we connected his reaction with sensations of tension and discomfort. He recalled that a few months previously, he had run a call for a shooting turned murder. The scene was quite gruesome, and the outcome was tragic. And guess where it all occurred? Yes, a grocery store. So, the next time he went into a grocery store, he was unconsciously triggered by the familiar sights and smells, and it brought up an overwhelming desire to leave. He didn't go back to a grocery store for over six months.

Again, connecting our sensations in the body with thoughts and emotions is how we move thoughts and emotions from the unconscious to the conscious. Connecting the body to the mind helps us sort through our own unconscious and sometimes unnoticeable chaos to find out what's really going on beneath it all. When we make these connections, we can do something to help alleviate our own suffering without going into emergency mode. Mindfulness interventions train us to see each breath we take, each new sound or sensation we notice, as the beginning of a new moment. By practicing TBT to become conscious of our thoughts, feelings, and situation, we reinforce our mental "muscle memory" that triggers do not have to end in dysregulation. Instead, fostering awareness creates a moment to reflect and adjust behaviors from reactive to responsive.

CONTEMPLATION QUESTIONS

Do any of your own triggers come to mind? Certain sounds, situations, people, smells? Can you list a few?

____

____

____

____

____

DON'T FORGET!

Fill out the first column of the self-assessment chart before practicing the mindfulness intervention.

Mindfulness Intervention Self-Assessment

SIGNALS

The self-assessment chart that follows is designed to track your progress. This chart will help you assess three things:

- How you feel before doing the mindfulness intervention, from 1 = you feel your best to 5 = you feel your worst
- How you feel after doing the mindfulness intervention, from 1 = you feel your best to 5 = you feel your worst
- How you felt while practicing the mindfulness intervention, from 1 = it was pleasant to 5 = it was unpleasant

Fill out the first column of the chart *before* you move on to the mindfulness intervention practice in this chapter. *After* you've practiced the intervention, fill out the second and third columns.

Remember that these assessments are subjective. There are no right or wrong answers and no judgment. And make it easy on yourself—write it down directly in the book, and you can always come back to it for reference.

MINDFULNESS INTERVENTION SELF-ASSESSMENT

Pre-assessment	Post-assessment	Summary Assessment
Overall Mood/Quality (1 = Best → 5 = Worst)	Overall Mood/Quality (1 = Best → 5 = Worst)	Quality of Intervention (1 = Pleasant → 5 = Unpleasant)

Mindfulness Intervention

SIGNALS

This practice trains the brain to identify sensations in the body (pain, vibration, pressure), which then develops the ability to connect those sensations with thoughts and/or emotions. Training the brain to notice and make these connections helps create awareness when we are triggered or activated by something in the environment, which then cultivates the ability to pivot our thinking to something that calms the nervous system, like breathing or listening. Sometimes our bodies react before our mind is aware. When you train yourself to notice your body reacting, it then informs you that you have something you need to pay attention to.

How to Practice

Set a timer for practicing or do what feels comfortable for you.

1. **Find a comfortable seated position.** Sit in a way that is comfortable but not too relaxed. You should have a feeling of sitting upright but not "uptight." Allow your eyes to close or keep them open and focused on a single point.
2. **Imagine/feel.** Bring to mind the following situations. Think about the idea/concept, visualize it, and then see if you can tap into where you feel it in the body:
    a. *Hunger:* Imagine you are hungry, really think about what it feels like right before you are ready to eat. Now be curious. How do you know you are actually hungry? What information does your body share with you to tell you that you are hungry? Do you picture food? Does your mouth begin to water? Do you feel an emptiness in your stomach? Notice whatever sensation you have and connect the idea of hunger to that feeling.
    b. *Fatigue:* Now imagine you are tired, really think about what it feels like right before you are ready to fall asleep. How do you know you are tired? What information does your body have

that is connected to fatigue? Maybe you picture your bed and your head resting on a pillow. Or maybe you feel like you want to yawn. Or your body sinks a little into the chair and your eyes begin to feel heavy. Notice sensations you have in your body and connect those with the idea of feeling sleepy or fatigued.

c. *Joy:* Pivot to picturing or thinking about something that brings you joy. This could be a pet, a past vacation, an upcoming cookout, gardening, or going for a hike. Tell yourself a little story about the experience. Now be curious about how it makes you feel. How do you know you are happy? Do you feel light? Or does the thought put a smile on your face or make the corners of your eyes lift? Maybe you feel a sense of warmth in your belly, even a sense of happiness in your heart.

d. *Annoyance:* Now change your image to that of something that is slightly irritating. Nothing traumatic, just a situation in the future or past that is slightly annoying. How do you know you are annoyed? Do you replay the situation over and over in your head? Do you tell yourself stories about it? Do you picture the people or events? See if you can connect the image with a sensation. Where does your body feel annoyance or irritation? Do you feel your eyebrows furrow? Or is your jaw clenching? Or are your hands suddenly balled up in fists? Maybe you even feel heat rise in your chest up to your neck. Or your breathing becomes shallow.

e. *Joy:* Finally, think back to that experience/situation that brought you joy. See if you can recall not only the situation but the connected feeling: lightness, smile, calm, warm. Ask yourself, *Where do I feel joy?* Bring yourself back to that emotion. Breathe, feel joy in your body, and sit with the feeling that it cultivates.

3. **Three closing breaths.** Once you have practiced for a comfortable amount of time, take three deep closing breaths, exhaling longer than inhaling. Bring your attention to your feet on the ground and think about what they feel like. Take one more breath and open your eyes, or just refocus on the room.

Mindfulness Intervention QR Code: Guided Signals

You can check out a recorded guided practice here:

Mindfulness Intervention Self-Assessment

Return to the self-assessment chart to fill out the postassessment and summary assessment columns *after* you practice the mindfulness intervention.

CHAPTER 7

CREATING NEW HABITS

"We are what we repeatedly do.
Excellence, then, is not an act, but a habit."

– Will Durant

In this chapter, I will address:

- Chief Smith's story of habitual patterns becoming unhealthy
- The concept of habits
- How mindfulness helps identify bad habits and redirects toward healthy habits
- Mindfulness intervention: **Naming**

NOTICING AND CHANGING HABITS

Fire Chief Smith is a retired military veteran who boxed on the U.S. Army boxing team for five years before going into fire services. He is very regimented in all things and feels most comfortable when he has a predictable routine. Every night, after he leaves work, he spends 45 minutes commuting the 10 miles to his home. By the time he walks in the door, he's suffering from a vague unsettled feeling. Whether it was because of the traffic, an annoying interaction he had with a subordinate, an unusually busy day, or a traumatic call he went on, his arrival at home never quite brings the comfort he's looking for. So he relies on something that unconsciously creates a sense of safety and comfort: food.

The pattern looks the same every night: Chief Smith walks through the door, puts his bag on the hall table, places his keys on the wall hook, yells to his wife, "Hey hon, I'm home," and heads straight to the kitchen. Like clockwork, he opens the refrigerator and pulls out the previous night's leftovers, or whatever else is readily available. The time of day or night doesn't matter, nor does it matter if he's had lunch or even if he feels hungry. Oftentimes, he does not even realize he's eating until he's halfway through the contents of the container. All he knows is that, after a hard day at work, the very act of eating seems to bring a sense of routine and comfort that makes him feel better.

FOOD FOR THE SOUL

Our brain makes connections between events based on a **feedback loop**, where engaging in a behavior creates a tendency to repeat the behavior in the future. Sometimes the feedback loop has positive effects, sometimes negative. Unfortunately, regardless of whether the effects help us or hurt us, the familiarity of the feedback loop is what reinforces it. This is because our brain interprets "familiar" as comfortable, predictable, and safe.

You may have observed this type of feedback loop in action with family members or friends. For example, let's say your friend is creating some unnecessary drama. Even though you consider their problem to be overblown, you try to be a good friend by comforting them and showing empathy for their situation. However, receiving attention only encourages your friend to continue creating drama in the future. (We all know that person!)

Cycles like this also occur with our own behavior. We misconstrue a feeling that was made through a leap rather than a direct connection and end up falsely identifying something as a fix, even when it's not. Let's talk food cravings as an example. When eating something you enjoy—say, a piece of chocolate cake—the brain bookmarks the pleasant feelings you experience (*Yummy flavor! Sugar buzz!*) as evidence that you are doing something "good." So far, not a horrible thing. It does feel good to eat cake—no shame in that! But where things get misconstrued is in the neurological connection your brain makes between the good feelings of eating cake and the bad feelings you might have from something completely unrelated.

This has been Chief Smith's experience too. He comes home from a long day at work, a day filled with stress, chaos, and trauma. When he walks in the door, his emotional state is *I feel like crap*. His processing brain jumps into the conversation and says, *I know what will make you feel better: food! And there is leftover cake in the fridge.* Because his brain has connected eating with a positive change in mood, Chief Smith, without even thinking about it, walks straight to the refrigerator. The feedback loop went from *I like cake* to *Cake makes me feel good* to *I feel like crap, but cake has made me feel good in the past* to *Cake will make me feel better again*. All the processing happens in less time than it took you to read this sentence.

Accidental Reinforcement

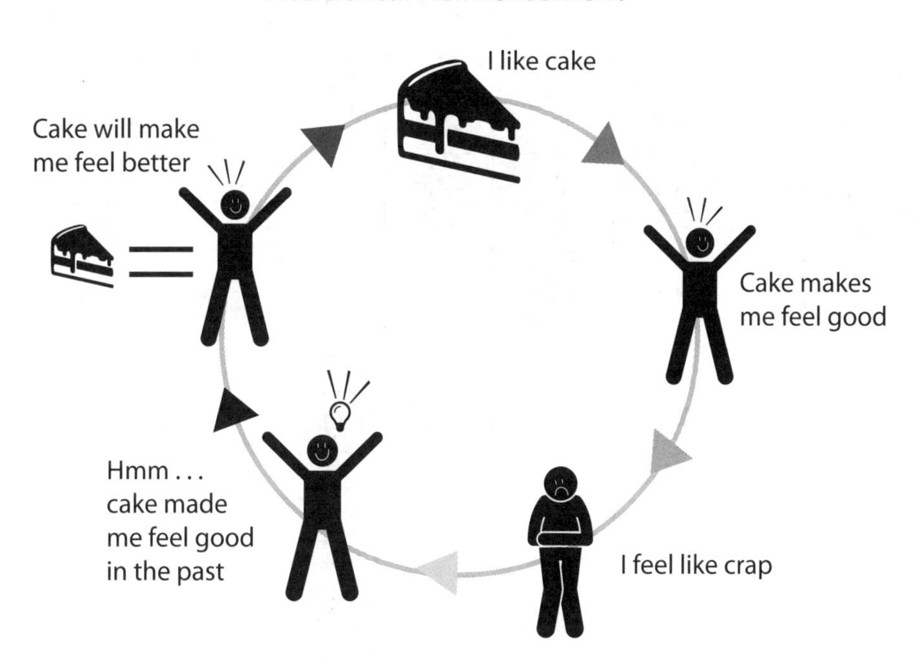

MINDS CHANGE BODIES, BODIES CHANGE MINDS

Creating a feedback loop typically happens unconsciously. The brain responds to positive or negative stimuli and creates habits based on a behavioral outcome—you remained safe, you got what you wanted, you felt better. It makes sense, then, that awareness is needed in order to break a feedback loop so you can create a new positive habit.

The first step is to identify the behavior/habit you would like to change. Sometimes habits are glaringly obvious, but others can be hard to nail down. You may know you feel horrible in the morning, but you may not realize it's from habitually falling asleep on the couch every night. Or you might be a little overweight, but you have not connected it to habitual stress-eating before bed. Reflecting on your daily activities over a week or two can help you identify the root behavior or habit behind the problem that you want to change. Once you have identified the root behavior or habit, you can then identify triggers that lead to that behavior or habit. Looking at patterns over a few weeks helps create a picture of which behaviors/habits to keep and which ones to change.

How do you feel after performing behavior/habit?

Behavior/ habit	SUN	MON	TUE	WED	THU	FRI	SAT
Sleep	☺	☺	☹				
Unhealthy food	☹	☺	☺				
Exercise	☺	☹	☺				
Alcohol	☹	☺	☺				

Use the following chart to fill in your own behavior/habit patterns and associated outcomes.

How do you feel after performing behavior/habit?

Behavior/ habit	SUN	MON	TUE	WED	THU	FRI	SAT

Connecting what is occurring (information from the brain) to our physical or mental feeling (information from the body) helps us identify what to keep and what needs to change. Our bodies hold a ton of information when we pay attention to what we're feeling. But during times of stress, correctly assessing those feelings can be difficult. As we saw in the last chapter, identifying a physical state can help us identify a mental state. TBT helps us tune into the body to establish this connection. When we tune into our bodies and connect with what is occurring physically, we can use these moments to inform a mental reaction:

- *My hands are in fists; I must be upset about something.*
- *I feel like running away; I must be stressed about something.*
- *My stomach is upset; I must have anxiety about something.*

Then you can ask yourself, *I wonder what happened just prior to this physical reaction?* This approach can help identify both the emotion and what triggered it, which then leads you to the behavior/habit that typically follows. Once you have figured out your behaviors/habits and the triggers behind them, you can move to the next phase: linking a known action to a new behavior that replaces the bad habit.

In his book *Atomic Habits*, James Clear discusses the concept of **stacking habits** as a way to create new and beneficial habits.* Rather than getting caught up in trying to disappear a bad habit, you instead replace the behavior with something healthy. The concept is to connect an existing behavior or action, something you already do each day, with a new behavior that replaces an unwanted behavior.

For example, I worked with someone who was an avid smoker. He would take numerous breaks during the workday to go outside and smoke a cigarette, even in rain, snow, or a heatwave. This habit meant his day was continually disrupted, not to mention the smoker's cough he had for over a year. Nevertheless, the thought of not smoking was overwhelming for him. So rather than focus on *not smoking*, he instead replaced smoking with something he enjoyed, and connected the replacement with an existing behavior (i.e., he stacked a new behavior). Here's what this process looked like:

- He would feel the desire to smoke, which would lead him to get up and walk outside—his usual habit.
- Since he loved reading but never had time for it, he decided to stack "grabbing a book to read" on top of "get up and walk outside."
- Going forward, every time he would feel the need to smoke, he'd get up and begin to walk outside, grab his book on the way out, and instead of smoking, he would sit and read.

Replacing smoking with reading—a pretty good trade-off, don't you think? As you can imagine, this didn't change things immediately, but he began to build neural pathways away from a desire to smoke and toward a desire to read. It took his body some time to adjust, but eventually he quit smoking and used the found time to enjoy a hobby he missed. Win-win!

Let's come back to Chief Smith. Once he realized what was behind his habit of mindlessly snacking to make himself feel better, he began making changes in his routine when he got home from work. Looking at the patterns within his routine, Chief Smith was able to find moments when he could redirect and link an existing action to a new action that would replace the bad habit.

---

* Clear, J. (2018). *Atomic habits: An easy & proven way to build good habits & break bad ones*. Avery.

TACTICAL BRAIN TRAINING IN ACTION

Scenario: Chief Smith arrives home at the end of a very stressful day.

Awareness: He knows his habit.

Internal Signal: As he walks in the door, he can already feel discomfort.

Amygdala: Uh-oh! Hurry, do something! I know—shove some food in your mouth!

PFC: [A little clueless.] Head to the fridge. It's filled with comfort!

Mindfulness in Action:

- Awareness: *It's been a hard, long day, and I really feel low.*
- Paying attention: *I feel the need to do something to alleviate this uncomfortable feeling.*
- Present moment: *What am I feeling? Am I hungry? No, not really. I'm tired and I need to chill and resource right now.*
- Non-judgmentally: *Crap, I was automatically heading for the refrigerator. No big deal, though . . . and great job noticing it!*

Mindfulness Intervention: *Maybe if I tune into what my body feels like right now, I can refocus and pivot. Hmm. I think I feel unsatisfied.*

PFC: Considering that I feel unsatisfied, I wonder what I can do to create some satisfaction. And how can I incorporate this prior to reaching unconsciously for food? Here's a plan I think we can accomplish:

- Walk through the door: *I can still do that.*
- Put bag on the hall table: *Easy.*
- Place keys on the wall hook: *I could use this as my link!*
- ~~Head straight to kitchen.~~
- **Replacement:** Pick up the mail that is next to the key hook.
    - *The mail looks interesting. In fact, I really enjoy looking through the mail.*
- ~~Unconsciously eat.~~
- **New Habit:** Sit in front room and sort through the mail.
    - Reading and sorting the mail creates ease and comfort.

Amygdala: I don't really detect an emergency here.

PFC: Let the rest of the body know we are smooth sailing, discomfort alleviated. I'm chillin' and reading. No need to feed the beast!

PRACTICING MINDFULNESS

Mindfulness teaches us to specifically notice a feeling that is associated with a particular habit, illuminate the habit while it is occurring, and then replace the harmful behavior with something helpful. Think about the desire to eat, for example. Is it because you're responding to a sensation of hunger, or are you mindlessly reacting out of habit? Maybe you feel an empty sensation in your stomach. That could indicate hunger. Or is it maybe an uncomfortable feeling? Or is it a restless feeling? Or do you just feel bored? Is it possible you think you are hungry, but in actuality you are trying to fill a need or make yourself feel better?

Asking curious questions like these is an important concept that mindfulness is attuned to. The idea is to cultivate what is called **beginner's mind**. When you are a beginner at something, you see things with fresh eyes, as if the situation has arrived for the first time. And because it is the first time, the outcome of the situation is unknown. No assumptions, no predecided conclusions. During moments of "hunger," for instance, you can apply this approach. Rather than assume the uncomfortable feeling in your gut is hunger, instead be curious about the circumstance around it: What is the sensation, why are you feeling it, and what healthy action could you take to alleviate or settle it?

As you become more aware, you will consciously identify sensations around unhealthy habits and notice a desire to engage with them. Mindfulness trains you to put your mind in your body by noticing unhealthy habits and put your body in your mind by taking an action that calms your nervous system, so that you can consciously choose to discard unhealthy behaviors and create new and healthier habits.

CONTEMPLATION QUESTIONS

Think of a habit you have. When do you engage in that habit? What do you think you are feeling that makes you want to engage in that habit? How does the habit serve you? Where and when in your day do you perform an unhealthy habit?

____

____

____

What triggers do you have that lead to the habit? Put an extra focus on activities/actions you perform prior to the habit.

____

____

____

What physical sensations do you feel prior to engaging in the habit (heat rising in face/neck, squeezing fists, clenching jaw)?

____

____

____

What mental sensations do you feel prior to engaging in the habit (ruminating, spinning negative thoughts, anger, sadness)?

____

____

____

What existing behavior/action do you take, prior to the unhealthy habit, that can be used as your link?

____

____

____

DON'T FORGET!

Fill out the first column of the self-assessment chart before practicing the mindfulness intervention.

Mindfulness Intervention Self-Assessment

NAMING

The self-assessment chart that follows is designed to track your progress. This chart will help you assess three things:

- How you feel before doing the mindfulness intervention, from 1 = you feel your best to 5 = you feel your worst
- How you feel after doing the mindfulness intervention, from 1 = you feel your best to 5 = you feel your worst
- How you felt while practicing the mindfulness intervention, from 1 = it was pleasant to 5 = it was unpleasant

Fill out the first column of the chart *before* you move on to the mindfulness intervention practice in this chapter. *After* you've practiced the intervention, fill out the second and third columns.

Remember that these assessments are subjective. There are no right or wrong answers and no judgment. And make it easy on yourself—write it down directly in the book, and you can always come back to it for reference.

MINDFULNESS INTERVENTION SELF-ASSESSMENT

Pre-assessment	Post-assessment	Summary Assessment
Overall Mood/Quality (1 = Best → 5 = Worst)	Overall Mood/Quality (1 = Best → 5 = Worst)	Quality of Intervention (1 = Pleasant → 5 = Unpleasant)

Mindfulness Intervention

NAMING

This practice can help you identify your triggers to habits and ramp down reactive mind states. You will learn to identify feelings and thoughts as they arise, so you can reduce and de-escalate automatic reactions. When you name an emotion (e.g., *This is anger* or *This is frustration*), you create more space to choose how to respond to the situation at hand.

How to Practice

Set a timer for practicing or do what feels comfortable for you.

1. **Find a seated position.** Sit in a way that is comfortable but not too relaxed. You should have a feeling of sitting upright but not "uptight." Allow your eyes to close or keep them open and focused on a single point.
2. **Notice your breath.** Bring your attention to how you are breathing. There is no right or wrong way to breathe, just breathe naturally. After a few breaths, begin to slow your inhales and exhales.
3. **Notice your thoughts.** As you breathe, you will notice that your mind wanders. Thoughts will come and go. Don't worry; this is normal.
4. **Name your thoughts.** When you become aware of a thought, try naming it. For example, if you start thinking about something stressful at work, say to yourself, *Stress*. If you notice an uncomfortable sensation in your body, say to yourself, *Pain*. Other labels might include distraction, impatience, anxiety, judgment, fear, and so on.
5. **Return to your breath.** After you give a name to the thought, guide your awareness back to your breathing. When your mind wanders again (and it will!), name it again and come back to your breath.
6. **Three closing breaths.** Once you have practiced for a comfortable amount of time, take three deep closing breaths, exhaling longer than inhaling. Bring your attention to your feet on the ground and think

about what they feel like. Take one more breath and open your eyes, or just refocus on the room.

Mindfulness Intervention QR Code: Guided Naming

You can check out a recorded guided practice here:

Mindfulness Intervention Self-Assessment

Return to the self-assessment chart to fill out the postassessment and summary assessment columns *after* you practice the mindfulness intervention.

CHAPTER 8

RECOGNIZING RUMINATION

"It is well to remember that the entire universe, with one trifling exception, is composed of others."

– John Holmes

In this chapter, I will address:

- Diane and Brian's story of being pulled from duty during an internal investigation
- Rumination (overfocus and attention on stressful thoughts)
- How mindfulness helps identify ruminating thoughts and redirect to healthy thoughts
- Mindfulness intervention: **Negative, Neutral, Positive**

SPLIT SECOND

It happened in a split second. They moved into action, took care of business, and didn't think about it again until the suspect was in custody. The two officers, Diane and Brian, had worked nights together for well over a year and completely trusted one another. On this night, Diane and Brian were called to a robbery in progress. They arrived on scene to a dimly lit two-story house in a quiet neighborhood. As they entered the house through the back door, the suspect immediately saw them, pulled out a gun, and aimed it directly at them. On instinct and training, one of the officers pulled their side arm and fired, hitting the suspect. The suspect was taken to the hospital and arrested. He was eventually convicted.

No matter the situation, according to protocol when an officer fires their service weapon on the job, they are automatically taken off the streets during the internal review process. Over the next four months, Diane and Brian had a lot of downtime, doing paperwork and other desk duty tasks. During this time, both officers found themselves repeatedly contemplating the incident. Because they were unable to discuss the case during the investigation process, both were left with their own memories, replaying every aspect of how it unfolded and thinking about how they could have done things better, criticizing, questioning, judging, and doubting their own actions.

Focused attention on stressful thoughts is known as **rumination**. Hard to identify and difficult to stop, rumination is often experienced as negative ideas, memories, or assessments replaying on a loop, over and over. It's a mentally dangerous cycle that can lead to feelings of self-doubt, inadequacy, and unworthiness.

When recalling the incident they'd been involved with, both Diane and Brian expressed similar ruminating thoughts that kept them up at night and led them to second-guess their behavior in every aspect of life:

Did I follow protocol?

I should have done things differently.

I shouldn't have pulled my firearm.

What if she had missed when she fired?

Why didn't we go in the side door instead?

Why didn't we call for backup before entering?

Why, why, why?

What if, what if, what if?

TRAUMA INGRAINS NEGATIVE CYCLES

Analyzing a situation or event is very important for self-reflection and situational investigation. In his book *Chatter*, Ethan Kross explains that this type of analytical thinking allows us "to hold information in our minds, reflect on our decisions, control our emotions, simulate alternative futures, reminisce about the past, keep track of our goals, and continually update the personal narratives that undergird our sense of who we are."* Paying attention to the voices in our head is key to relating to ourselves and the world. But when the voices become negative, taking over most other thoughts and spinning out of control, things can get ugly.

On one side of the overthinking spectrum, repetitive thoughts about something neutral or positive can simply be annoying. For example, you hear a song and then can't stop playing it in your head. But ruminating, the other side of the overthinking spectrum, can become mentally exhausting. It may look like a constant replay of a conversation that went awry, or a steady stream of images related to a traumatic event. Unlike positive or neutral thinking, which may provide insight and help create a strategy for what to do better next time, rumination leads to a decrease in cognitive function. Negative thoughts intensify feelings of stress, triggering the body to secrete cortisol, which, as mentioned in previous chapters, inhibits logic and rational thought. With this decrease in your ability to think clearly, you're left to simply focus on the negative thoughts, which makes you feel worse, and the rumination cycle continues on repeat.

The rumination cycle can be particularly hard to interrupt when it's set off by a traumatic experience. Anytime something out of the ordinary occurs, certain aspects of the situation become more ingrained in our memory. While we tend to not remember mundane everyday occurrences like what we had to eat last night or what we watched on TV last week, we can recall events like a painful accident, a dangerous encounter, or an argument with a partner in sharp detail, particularly the sensory details of the experience (sights, sounds, smells), as well as our split-second thoughts and emotions from one moment to the next. At the same time, trauma can make other parts of the memory harder to recall, like what order things happened in, or why we made certain decisions or took certain actions. This is because trauma, being an emergent situation, activates our survival brain while turning off our thinking brain. Once the experience is over, we're left to piece together a fragmented collection of images and sense memories.

The effort to make logical sense out of these fragmented memories only reinforces our attention to negative thoughts, usually about ourselves. Instead of dwelling on the fact that we survived or all the ways we did our best to manage the situation, we keep replaying our sensations of danger, self-judgment, and shame. It feels like

* Kross, E. (2021). *Chatter: The voice in our head, why it matters, and how to harness it*. Crown.

"learning" from the experience, but in fact, it's only magnifying our negative feelings and making the negative thought cycle even harder to manage.

Both Diane and Brian experienced trauma related to the on-the-job shooting. As a result, both questioned their memories of the incident and suffered from extreme self-judgment over how they handled it. Both wondered if they had followed protocol by announcing their presence while approaching the house. Brian, once inside and faced with the suspect, had not been able to pull his sidearm; to make matters worse, he had almost crossed Diane's line of fire. In addition to feelings of inadequacy and incompetence, he suffered from a surreal near-death feeling from having put his own life in danger. Diane, meanwhile, had been able to fire at the suspect; her shot had almost killed him. The thought of nearly taking someone's life weighed on her heavily. She also suffered from the knowledge that she'd come pretty close to shooting her partner instead; the thought of what could have happened was on constant replay in her mind.

Rumination about a traumatic experience doesn't just beget more rumination about it. Oftentimes, those negative thoughts spill over into other areas of life. Caught in their ruminative cycle of shame and self-judgment, both partners began to feel a sense of discontent and dysregulation, not only about their performance in the incident but about themselves and the world in general.

This is where rumination can become dangerous—the negative self-worth it fosters may progress to avoidance of processing the experience and our emotions around it. Without adequate processing of trauma, it becomes even easier for the brain to make potentially destructive leaps in logic. Analyses and conclusions about the experience may start with a basis in reality, only to spiral rapidly into conjecture.

For example, let's say you arrived on the scene of a traffic accident in which someone was trapped in their vehicle. You followed your training, but in the course of extracting them from the vehicle, they were severely hurt and had to be transported to the hospital for further care. Reality tells you that the accident occurred, the patient was injured, and they are now under hospital supervision and care. Meanwhile, though, your thoughts are lost in a spin cycle of conjecture: *I wonder how they are doing. I wonder if they survived. Could I have done something different? Did I cause further damage? Was I the cause of their death? Did I do my job properly? I did a poor job. I am not good at what I do. I am not good at anything. I suck at life. I just hope they're okay. I wonder how they are doing. I wonder if they survived.* On and on and on the spin cycle goes, entrenching us ever deeper in the rumination cycle and the self-judgment and shame it fosters. These negative feelings toward ourselves can lead us down a slippery slope of behavioral habits like depression, anxiety, worthlessness, and even isolation—all things that make us more prone to bad judgment calls, tactical mistakes, and harmful behavior on and off the job. Instead of healing and learning from the traumatic situation, we end up guaranteeing the result that brings us the most fear and shame.

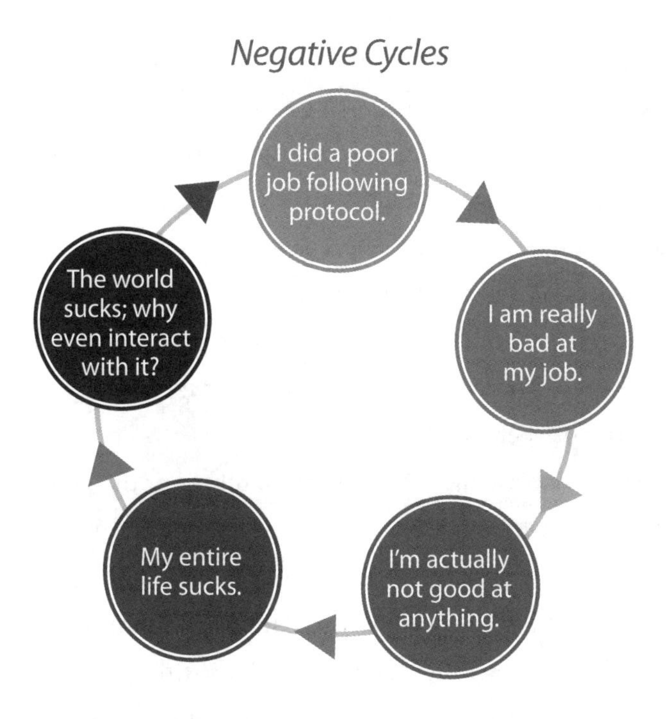

GETTING OUT OF THE SPIN CYCLE

There are two parts to stopping the rumination cycle. First comes **recognition**: noticing when you're in a spiral of thinking that doesn't serve you. Next comes **redirection**: shifting your thoughts to something either neutral or positive. Mindfulness helps with both, teaching us to notice when a thought is on repeat and empowering us to press the pause button, stop the downward spiral, and tune into another thought.

Recognition comes through training to identify when the rabbit hole of rumination is calling your name. Paying attention to your inner monologue can help. When you're having a thought that is accompanied by discomfort or signs that you're moving out of your window of tolerance, ask yourself, *Is this a thought I have had before? Am I hyperfocused on this?* If the answer is yes, it's time to interrupt and redirect.

In his book *Trauma-Sensitive Mindfulness*, David Treleaven discusses how a concept called **non-judgmental attention** can help us stop a negative cycle through mindfully focusing on neutral and positive thoughts. By bringing curiosity and acceptance to the negative thoughts that occur in the wake of trauma, non-judgmental attention offers a moment of reprieve in which we can think about our thoughts, rather than attach to them and allow them to define us. This ability makes us less reactive to negative thought spirals when they arise.*

Focusing—intentionally thinking about *this* and not *that*—is simple, but not easy. A lot of the time, we have no idea we are distracted. And when the distraction is a negative thought, it's even harder to redirect our brains away from it. The amygdala likes to hold on to those kinds of thoughts, making sure you remember them in order to keep you safe from repeating the (real or perceived) mistake again. But when you practice a mindfulness intervention, you're building the "muscle" of realization and redirection, making it easier for your brain to recognize when you're caught in a negative thought spiral (*Oh, there I go—I am ruminating*) and redirect your attention to a thought that is more beneficial for you.

If you notice while practicing the intervention that your thoughts are in a negative spiral or find your brain hijacked by a traumatic memory, you can easily interrupt the negativity by listening to the sounds in the room, taking a few deep breaths, or focusing on something that generates positive emotions. With repeated practice over time, this awareness will extend into your interactions with the world. Let's say you're in a conversation with someone, and their physical cues or facial expression send you down a path of negative self-talk: *They don't understand me; they are so defensive; why do I even try?* Thanks to the practice you've been doing, your brain remembers what "negative talk" feels like, and your training kicks in: You remember to redirect your thoughts and listen to sounds, take a breath, feel the ground beneath your feet, and bring yourself back into the present moment.

BACK IN THE SADDLE

It took four long months of boring desk work and intense internal reviews before Diane and Brian were cleared for duty and put back on the streets. Their downtime was occupied with a lot of worrying about losing their jobs, the negative perception

* Treleaven, D. A. (2018). *Trauma-sensitive mindfulness: Practices for safe and transformative healing*. W. W. Norton.

of their coworkers, and future job performance. The internal inquisition on constant loop in their heads contributed to a decline in both physical and mental health for both officers: poor eating habits, lack of motivation to exercise, apathy at work, and overall anxious feelings. Finally getting back on the streets was a beneficial disruption for both of them, but in order to truly recover their effectiveness as police officers, they needed to break the rumination cycle by replacing the bad thoughts with good ones.

TACTICAL BRAIN TRAINING IN ACTION

Scenario: After months on desk duty, Diane and Brian are back to working the streets again.

Awareness: Diane and Brian realize they have succumbed to a cycle of self-doubt and self-judgment. Diane is focused on thoughts of coworkers not trusting her and being annoyed at her, while Brian suffers from an anxious feeling of pins and needles all the time.

Amygdala: These thoughts are really bad. These feelings are horrible. Something must be dangerously wrong. This has to be an emergency.

PFC: I believe you, Amygdala. I'm going to leave it to you to take care of.

Mindfulness in Action:

- Awareness: *I can't seem to focus. Every time I try to do something, my mind keeps coming back to the same disruptive thoughts. My thoughts are spinning out of control, and I can't stop them.*
- Paying attention: *Are my thoughts negative? They seemed to be filled with self-doubt, worry, and insecurity.*
- Present moment: *What am I feeling? My body feels heavy, like I'm walking in quicksand. My breathing seems labored and constricted. Why do I keep doing this to myself?*
- Non-judgmentally: *Wow, I noticed that my thoughts were negative, and I was spinning out of control. And I noticed that my mind and body were being affected. Good job noticing! Now what?*

Mindfulness Intervention: *I need to redirect. Maybe if I pause for a moment and do an intervention that takes me out of my head and into something else, I can stop the negative cycle. I will redirect my thoughts to something I* *know brings me joy. I am going to think about my upcoming fishing trip and imagine what it will be like to be on a boat, sitting in the water, the sun on my face, enjoying a peaceful day.*

Amygdala: This feels nice. Seems like things are copacetic again. Emergency averted. We are good to go.

PFC: Hey body, this is no longer bad stress. Get back to focusing on what you were doing (the good stuff, not the bad stuff!) and don't worry about your coworkers' attitude. You got this!

PRACTICING MINDFULNESS

So much of mindfulness is about building the networks and capacity for awareness. Awareness helps us differentiate between positive, negative, and neutral thoughts and empowers us to focus on the ones that serve us. If you feel like you're stuck in a thought loop or having difficulty keeping your focus where you want it, it can be a sign that your brain is still convinced that things are emergent or dangerous. The solution is to pause, take a few deep breaths, become aware of the thoughts, and be curious about how a mindfulness intervention could help in this moment.

CONTEMPLATION QUESTIONS

What are some topics or thoughts that get under your skin? What happens when you think about them?

____

____

____

____

Do you have any thoughts that are on repeat, and once you start thinking about them you can't stop the cycle?

____

____

____

____

DON'T FORGET!

Fill out the first column of the self-assessment chart before practicing the mindfulness intervention.

Mindfulness Intervention Self-Assessment

NEGATIVE, NEUTRAL, POSITIVE

The self-assessment chart that follows is designed to track your progress. This chart will help you assess three things:

- How you feel before doing the mindfulness intervention, from 1 = you feel your best to 5 = you feel your worst
- How you feel after doing the mindfulness intervention, from 1 = you feel your best to 5 = you feel your worst
- How you felt while practicing the mindfulness intervention, from 1 = it was pleasant to 5 = it was unpleasant

Fill out the first column of the chart *before* you move on to the mindfulness intervention practice in this chapter. *After* you've practiced the intervention, fill out the second and third columns.

Remember that these assessments are subjective. There are no right or wrong answers and no judgment. And make it easy on yourself—write it down directly in the book, and you can always come back to it for reference.

MINDFULNESS INTERVENTION SELF-ASSESSMENT

Pre-assessment	Post-assessment	Summary Assessment
Overall Mood/Quality (1 = Best → 5 = Worst)	Overall Mood/Quality (1 = Best → 5 = Worst)	Quality of Intervention (1 = Pleasant → 5 = Unpleasant)

Mindfulness Intervention

NEGATIVE, NEUTRAL, POSITIVE

This practice helps develop awareness regarding spiraling negative thinking cycles. The awareness created then promotes more emotionally balanced thinking. By disrupting negative thought cycles, attention is then focused on identifying *what* the thought is, rather than engaging in the thought and becoming *consumed by* it. This allows the mind to naturally disengage, developing more emotionally balanced thoughts.

How to Practice

Set a timer for practicing or do what feels comfortable for you.

1. **Begin by choosing a posture that is comfortable for you.** Either sit in a way that is comfortable or stand against a wall. You should have a feeling of sitting or standing tall, in a way that creates a sense of being aware of your surroundings. Allow your eyes to close or keep them open and focused on a single point in front of you.
2. **Choose an anchor.** Begin by choosing an anchor: breathing, listening, sensing, square breathing. Settle into a comfortable pattern for a few rounds.
3. **Negative, neutral, or positive identification.** Begin to bring awareness to your thoughts. When thoughts arise, categorize them into one of three categories: negative, neutral, or positive. Negative thoughts can be those that are distressing or challenging, neutral thoughts are more mundane and innocuous, and positive thoughts are those that generate joy or contentment.
4. **Refocus on anchor.** Once the thought is categorized, refocus back on your initial anchor. Repeat as often as needed, for the duration of the practice.
5. **Three closing breaths.** Once you have practiced for a comfortable amount of time, take three deep closing breaths, exhaling longer than

inhaling. Bring your attention to your feet on the ground and think about what they feel like. Take one more breath and open your eyes, or just refocus on the room.

Mindfulness Intervention QR Code: Guided Negative, Neutral, Positive

You can check out a recorded guided practice here:

Mindfulness Intervention Self-Assessment

Return to the self-assessment chart to fill out the postassessment and summary assessment columns *after* you practice the mindfulness intervention.

CHAPTER 9

EMOTIONAL REGULATION

"Keep your eyes on the stars but remember
to keep your feet on the ground."

– Theodore Roosevelt

In this chapter, I will address:

- Tim's story of freezing at an inopportune time
- Regulating emotions
- How mindfulness helps modulate emotions within the window of tolerance
- Mindfulness intervention: **Volume Control**

BAD TIMING

Tim was excited to join his local PD at the age of 25. He came from a long line of first responders, and from a very young age he wanted to be a police officer. He was particularly excited about the tactical training aspects and sailed through the academy with flying colors. Top of his class and very well liked, he seemed well suited to the life of a police officer. But near the end of his training, he experienced a situation that made him question everything.

The lesson that day was taser training. The instructor opened with a warning: "Everyone will be tased by the end of training today." Tim was at first enthusiastic—another skill to learn and, he hoped, excel at. Then, suddenly, his mood shifted. A feeling of deep pressure surrounded his chest and spread throughout his entire body. He felt an overwhelming sense of dread, and that's when it happened: He froze. His thoughts began to swirl around the impact of being tased. How badly was it going to hurt? Would he pass out in pain? What would happen if he hit his head on the ground? What if he accidentally released his bladder? Tim could not take his eyes off the weapon, could not control the sudden onset of tremors, could not move, listen, or focus. His emotions were going haywire, and he was terrified. As a result, he never heard the lecture, never saw the demonstration, never learned the mechanics of the weapon or how to use it. The next thing Tim recalled was hearing his name and being told to stand up. It was his turn to be tased.

THE FOUR Fs

How many times have you heard someone say (or said yourself), "I am so stressed out I can't even think" or "Just give me a second to think!" As mentioned in previous chapters, when stress is high, the thinking part of the brain can shut down, making it difficult to focus and concentrate. Instead, the amygdala takes over with survival reactions like fight, flight, freeze, or fawn (FFFF):

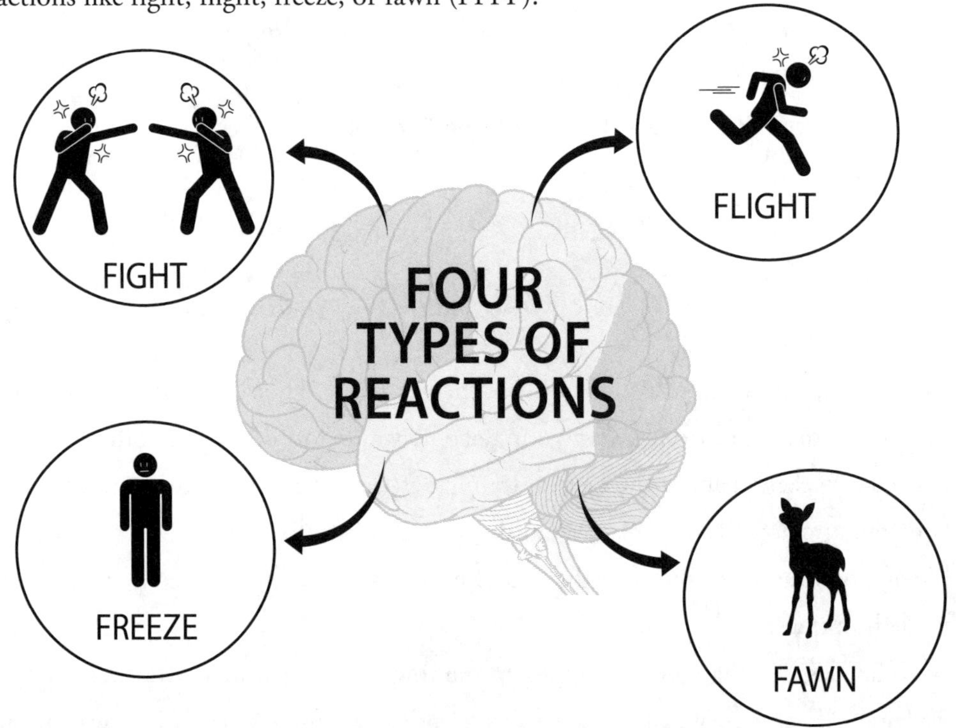

- **Fight:** You have assessed a situation and conclude (whether right or wrong) that you have the power to defeat your opponent.
- **Flight:** You have assessed a situation and decide that the antagonist can overpower you, so you run.
- **Freeze:** You have assessed a situation and conclude (unconsciously or consciously) that you can neither defeat nor run, so you freeze (hoping to blend into the background and go unnoticed).
- **Fawn:** You have assessed a situation and decide the best approach is to appease the threat through means such as codependency or a lack of boundaries.

Depending on the situation and how you are feeling, you can experience any of these reactions when confronting a perceived threat. You can even shift from one reaction to another during a single incident.

> *It's important to point out that each of these reactions is a normal response to high stress and that sometimes they can indeed save you (and may have saved you in the past). Fighting might be important if someone is threatening your life. Flight might be a great idea if you think you can get away from the situation. Freeze might be a great option if it means someone or something could pass you by unnoticed. Fawn might be the right tactic, feigning compliance while you wait out the storm. But when these reactions are in constant play, regardless of the situation's severity, the body and mind become exhausted. This leads to a physical or mental breakdown that depletes you of the resources needed to maintain a healthy lifestyle.*

BALANCING THE NERVOUS SYSTEM

These survival reactions aren't only triggered by high-stress or dangerous situations. Our bodies will also revert to FFFF when an overloaded mental state leaves us unable to balance emotions.

Emotional balance can deteriorate slowly over time or even in a split second. Typically, we are unaware of the deterioration that occurs, and the resulting imbalance may go unnoticed. Instead, these reactions often sneak up on us. One minute you're fine; the next, you find yourself in the middle of the reaction, or even coming to the realization after the fact.

Training our brains to notice these sliding moments helps manage mental overload and emotional imbalance. By training for awareness of our thoughts and emotions and identifying our edges, we can better manage our nervous system. If the nervous system is properly managed, control over emotions and actions naturally follows. And as we've seen, holding the reins of our emotions creates space for objective thinking, allowing for better external and internal relational communication and more effective problem-solving. By learning to modulate emotions before entering or (just as importantly) during FFFF, the mind and body become integrated, actively acknowledging an emotion and working with it, rather than becoming overwhelmed by it. This connection allows us to stay calm and focused during times of stress, sadness, anger. With that focus, we can determine if an FFFF reaction is in fact the right move and then do it with awareness and agency.

THE STORM AFTER THE STORM

Has anyone ever jumped out to surprise you? You can probably recall how that initial feeling of alarm didn't just go away once you realized what had occurred; it likely took a few minutes for your heartbeat to regulate and your nerves to calm down. This is similar to how our heightened emotions behave in the aftermath of an FFFF reaction. Just because the actual threat is over does not mean our brains have processed and accepted that fact. In his book *The Body Keeps the Score*, Dr. Bessel van der Kolk explains that sometimes even when a threat is over, survival reaction signals remain, and a continued secretion of stress hormone is expressed as agitation and panic, both of which can send your system out of balance.* The threat puts you over the edge of what is emotionally tolerable, and there you stay, body and mind on high alert, seeing every person and situation as a potential emergency or threat.

I spent some time working with a war veteran who struggled with this. He had experienced a high level of stress during a tumultuous childhood, which was replayed during his time in the army. As a result of living in a constant survival state for most of his youth and young adult life, it was only natural for him to expect that most

* Van der Kolk, B. (2014). *The body keeps the score: Brain, mind, and body in the healing of trauma*. Viking.

situations, even everyday ones, would be filled with stress and possibly emergent. Even when things were calm, he would unknowingly look for the stress points because he *knew* they were right around the corner.

This affected his life in two ways. First, treating everything as a threat meant having his guard up 24/7. The crying baby, the kid who was late coming home, the person who called in sick to work, the electricity that went out—all these situations, he believed, threatened dire consequences unless he took immediate and drastic action. That constant state of alert, looking around every corner, depleted him of energy, leaving him physically and emotionally exhausted all the time.

Second, he fell into a cycle of positively reinforcing a negative belief. He could preemptively assess five different situations as being emergent, and when just one of them proved to be a true emergency, he would then say, "See, I was right! I knew this situation was going to end badly!" Even though he'd been wrong four other times, the one real emergency reinforced his belief that danger was everywhere.

For this veteran, the cycle ran so deep that it impacted his ability to feel comfortable with being calm. Chaotic feelings were familiar, which made them feel safe and soothing to his brain—after all, he knew how to function in a state of chaos. But when life was quiet and copacetic, discomfort set in and he would unconsciously disturb the peace, creating issues when none existed. Naturally, this affected his relationships with people. Even a simple gesture of friendship was an occasion for distrust; as he explained it, he was always looking for the other person's "angle." With his emotions stuck in high alert, ready for FFFF, there was never a chance for him to feel settled or threats to feel resolved. Even when the storm was over, the stormy feelings never passed.

The next time you feel a shift in your mood, be curious about what is happening. If you notice any agitation or a desire to avoid something, a simple question can help focus your brain so that it can guide you to your next step: Is this a threat or a challenge? Am I surviving or thriving?

This approach does two things:

- *Redirects your thoughts toward focused attention and away from FFFF*
- *Provides some needed clarity to the situation (just in case you actually do have to run!)*

ZONED OUT

Let's get back to Tim, the police academy trainee. Overwhelmed with fear of the pain he thought he would endure from being tased, his emotions were on steroids as he subconsciously evaluated his options:

- *Fight:* He could not fight his instructor to avoid being tased. It was inevitable.
- *Flight:* There was no way he could leave the classroom without embarrassment and possibly being penalized.
- *Fawn:* He could not talk his way out of the situation. This was a mandatory training.
- *Freeze:* He could stay put and "zone out" until the situation was over.

Tim's brain decided freezing was the best option (i.e., the least embarrassing). At the very least, it would keep him in the room, appearing to learn the lesson. But even as he stayed in his seat with his eyes fixed on the instructor, Tim's freeze reaction was far from calm. Thrown outside his window of tolerance, he mentally checked out of the situation, which brought the unfortunate outcome of losing time and valuable information from the lecture. When he was called on, he robotically got up, staring off into space as his body braced for the pain. When instead they asked him to fire the weapon rather than receive the tasing, Tim still couldn't respond. He told me he had no idea what to do: where to stand, how to hold the taser, or where to aim it on the other person. Even though his body had stayed in the classroom, his mind had exited hours ago.

Training to notice signs of FFFF can bring thinking back online, stop the downward cycle, and allow for a present body and mind. Bringing awareness to thoughts in the moment can help the brain discern whether something is a threat or simply uncomfortable. Just the act of identifying something as discomfort can keep you inside your window of tolerance, allowing you to regulate an emotion, stay reasonably connected to the situation you're in, and mentally focus on the task you are there to complete.

TACTICAL BRAIN TRAINING IN ACTION

Scenario: Tim is sitting in the training room at the police academy and realizes the pain he's about to undergo.

Awareness: The training has begun, and Tim is initially excited. Then his mood shifts.

Internal Signal: He starts to feel a deep pressure surrounding his chest.

Amygdala: SOMETHING BAD IS ABOUT TO HAPPEN. I just know it! YOU ARE IN DANGER. Literally. You are about to be TASED!

PFC: [Frozen.]

Mindfulness in Action:

- Awareness: *I feel out of control right now. I can't focus on the instructor or the lesson. I feel like I'm out of my window of tolerance.*
- Paying attention: *I should pause and take a look at what I am feeling and sensing right now.*
- Present moment: *Wow, my palms are super sweaty, and I feel like I have tunnel vision.*
- Non-judgmentally: *I feel like such a wimp right now. Wait. I am supposed to just notice what I feel, not judge it. Okay. Glad I was able to notice. Good job! Now get down to business.*

Mindfulness Intervention: *I am hyperfocused on my beating heart. I should turn the volume down on my panic feeling and turn the volume up on slow and long exhales, because I remember that a long exhale slows the heart.*

Amygdala: It seems like other people in class are able to manage being tased. No one is dying. Maybe it's not that bad. PFC, I think it's time for you to make some decisions.

PFC: I got this. We need to listen to the lecture and take some notes so we know what to expect.

PRACTICING MINDFULNESS

Mindfulness teaches us to create awareness when a shift in emotions occurs. The awareness helps the mind recognize sensations associated with strong feelings, then recall a mindfulness tool that can help regulate the brain and body and bring us back into the window of tolerance, where we can regain emotional balance. Simple awareness of our stress reactions—*I want to fight, I want to run, I want to freeze, I want to appease*—begins the process of regulating away from a distressed emotional response and toward a strategy for calming the nervous system, which allows the brain to resume executive functioning and process information accurately.

Strong emotions will always be part of life. While mindfulness does not eliminate the possibility of getting knocked down by these emotions, it does train the brain to modulate our emergency reactions and recover from them. The more we practice, the more we decrease the time it takes between getting hit by a strong emotion (going into FFFF) and coming back to a manageable state. You are able to right yourself faster, balance your emotions, and come back to your window of tolerance, where you can respond rather than react.

CONTEMPLATION QUESTIONS

Think of an example when you were hyperfocused on something. Did you experience a fight, flight, freeze, or fawn response?

____

____

____

____

How long did it take for you to recover?

____

____

____

____

DON'T FORGET!

Fill out the first column of the self-assessment chart before practicing the mindfulness intervention.

Mindfulness Intervention Self-Assessment

VOLUME CONTROL

The self-assessment chart that follows is designed to track your progress. This chart will help you assess three things:

- How you feel before doing the mindfulness intervention, from 1 = you feel your best to 5 = you feel your worst
- How you feel after doing the mindfulness intervention, from 1 = you feel your best to 5 = you feel your worst
- How you felt while practicing the mindfulness intervention, from 1 = it was pleasant to 5 = it was unpleasant

Fill out the first column of the chart *before* you move on to the mindfulness intervention practice in this chapter. *After* you've practiced the intervention, fill out the second and third columns.

Remember that these assessments are subjective. There are no right or wrong answers and no judgment. And make it easy on yourself—write it down directly in the book, and you can always come back to it for reference.

MINDFULNESS INTERVENTION SELF-ASSESSMENT

Pre-assessment	Post-assessment	Summary Assessment
Overall Mood/Quality (1 = Best → 5 = Worst)	Overall Mood/Quality (1 = Best → 5 = Worst)	Quality of Intervention (1 = Pleasant → 5 = Unpleasant)

Mindfulness Intervention

VOLUME CONTROL

This practice trains the brain to identify when emotions have hit the edge of what is tolerable and how to navigate back to safety by turning the volume up or down. It teaches us to notice what thoughts of *ease* and *unease* feel like, modulate between those emotional states, and settle on the side of ease, dialing up emotions of joy and contentment.

How to Practice

Set a timer for practicing or do what feels comfortable for you.

1. **Find a comfortable position.** Either sit in a way that is comfortable or stand against a wall. You should have a feeling of sitting or standing tall, in a way that creates a sense of being aware of your surroundings. Allow your eyes to close or keep them open and focused on a single point in front of you.
2. **Choose an anchor.** Begin by choosing an anchor: breathing, listening, sensing, square breathing. Settle into a comfortable pattern for a few rounds.
3. **Bring to mind a happy emotion.** Picture or think about something that brings you joy. A good book, an upcoming get together, listening to music, being outdoors. Drop into where or how you feel joy. Take it a step further and see if you can feel the emotion a little stronger, as if you can turn the volume up a notch.
4. **Bring to mind a stressful emotion.** Now change your image to that of something that creates stress (nothing dire or traumatizing). A missed work assignment, an argument with a coworker, traffic, an annoying neighbor. Think about where in your body you feel the stress. Do your shoulders tighten, or does your stomach feel sick? Now see if you can go a little deeper into the stress (but nothing traumatic).

5. **Modulate the volume.** Finally, think back to that experience/situation that brought you joy. See if you can turn the volume down on stress by recalling not only the situation but the feeling in your body connected with joy: lightness, smile, calm, warm. Ask yourself, *Where do I feel joy?* If you have a stressful thought again, bring yourself back to joy. Breathe, feel joy in your body, and sit with the felt feeling. Turn the dial on your connected feelings and see if you can feel deeper and stronger emotions connected with happiness. Every time your mind wanders, or if you have stressful thoughts, turn the volume down. Bring your attention back to thoughts of joy and see if you can turn the volume up on those associated feelings. Continue to modulate down on stress and up on joy for as long as comfortable.
6. **Three closing breaths.** Once you have practiced for a comfortable amount of time, take three deep closing breaths, exhaling longer than inhaling. Bring your attention to your feet on the ground and think about what they feel like. Take one more breath and open your eyes, or just refocus on the room.

Mindfulness Intervention QR Code: Guided Volume Control

You can check out a recorded guided practice here:

Mindfulness Intervention Self-Assessment

Return to the self-assessment chart to fill out the postassessment and summary assessment columns *after* you practice the mindfulness intervention.

CHAPTER 10

SELF-JUDGMENT

"Stop acting so small.
You are the universe in ecstatic motion."

– Rumi

In this chapter, I will address:

- Joan's story of having difficulty recovering from a tragic rescue
- Self-judgment
- How mindfulness helps recognize negative thinking and judging
- Mindfulness intervention: **Non-Judgmental Awareness**

WATCHING FROM THE TOWER

Joan is a retired beach lifeguard who worked for more than 20 years at an especially active area of the beach that attracted swimmers, boogie boarders, body surfers, and surfers. Over the course of her employment, she rescued hundreds of people from drowning and helped with numerous water and beach injuries. But as with any emergency career as long as Joan's, there were also some failures. Her most tragic rescue happened on what she originally thought was a calm day. With the crowd in the water made up of mostly local surfers, this would normally be a day where she could relax a little, knowing they were experienced swimmers. But then conditions changed. The waves grew large, the currents became unpredictable. Joan's attention shifted, and she became extra vigilant in her monitoring of the water.

One surfer caught her eye. He was a young kid, about 14 years old, whom she'd enjoyed watching over the years. He was smooth, agile, able to ride whatever wave the ocean presented, regardless of shape or size. Joan saw the boy catch the top of a particularly steep wave, then drop suddenly, with the wave crashing over him. She kept watching and eventually saw the surfer's head above water, but something didn't sit right with Joan. When she noticed that the boy's head was bobbing up and down in the water, she immediately knew something was wrong. She ran down the ramp, into the water, and swam as fast as she could. As she was swimming out, she watched as the boy slowly fell beneath the surface of the water. Just as she reached him, he was completely submerged.

Joan had trained for situations like this and knew exactly what to do. She dove down, grabbed the boy, pulled him up, and swam back to shore, keeping the boy's head above water as much as she could with the rough ocean continually crashing down on them both. By the time they reached shore, Joan was exhausted. But she could not stop—once her feet finally hit the sand, she ran, dragging the boy from the water to a flat area on the beach. She performed CPR and was able to get a pulse, only to realize things were worse than she had thought. The boy was now breathing and alert, but he was unable to move.

While Joan did save his life, the boy had broken his neck when his head hit the surfboard, and his injury led to permanent paralysis from the neck down. This final diagnosis hit Joan like a ton of bricks. Could she have prevented it? Should she have held the boy differently while swimming him in? Could she have secured his neck while pulling him to shore and still had time to resuscitate him? These thoughts led to a cycle of self-judgment that left her in immense suffering for years to come.

IF ONLY

Sometimes it's hard to manage feelings surrounding traumatic events and outcomes, especially when there is a feeling of associated fault. As an emergency responder, or even a bystander who steps in to help, it's important to remember that a traumatic situation often leads to unfortunate outcomes. For someone in a lifesaving position like Joan's, showing up, doing their job, and caring for others as best they can is the only expectation. But knowing that does not make it easy to separate our actions from a situation's outcome. Moving away from feelings of guilt and self-judgment—the "what-ifs" and "if-onlys"—and transitioning to acceptance can be very difficult.

Part of this shift begins with recognizing our inherent limitations. Rescues are complex, and no training can prepare us for every possible situation. The procedure for CPR can be taught, but the different circumstances where it's required are impossible to predict: on the roof of a burning house, in a car that is upside down, while running in a war zone, during a jail fight, on the phone with an emergency caller, and so many other situations that have been shared with me over the years. Decision-making must be done on the fly, without knowing what the outcome will be. When the dust settles, acceptance that we're doing the best we can do, given the circumstances and what we bring to the table, allows our brains and bodies to recover so that we can continue bringing our best to the next situation.

ALLOWING FOR ACCEPTANCE

When we're assessing the outcome of a situation, our brain often slips into judgment mode. We make assumptions and develop opinions about situations, people, and even ourselves all day long. Judgment is normal and can even be beneficial when we're looking at an incident to learn from the outcome. For instance, assessing that it was *not* a good idea to put your hand on an open flame and learning that this action will have negative consequences is a great use of judgment. But when the brain uses judgment in a way that prevents you from accepting the outcome, your processing of the incident can become compromised.

As we've discussed already, our brain is wired to notice failures and mistakes as a way of keeping us from repeating dangerous situations. But falling into and placing blame on ourselves for the outcome (*I should have X; I wish I would have Y*) can be damaging to our mental health, launching us into a negative thought cycle like the kind we discussed in chapter 8. Acceptance means looking at a past event and acknowledging its impact without connecting yourself to it. It does not mean you like the outcome or even agree with it, but that you are allowing it to exist.

Acceptance depends on changing the relationship between stimulus and outcome in the brain. As mentioned in chapter 5, a stimulus can be anything: a car cutting you off, a child being a brat, bills that must be paid, a violent outburst by a suspect, a patient that didn't make it, a coworker you don't get along with. These things will always be part of life, and it's rarely possible to predict them. The only things that can be changed are how you relate to the stimulus and the self-imposed connection you make with its outcome. Falling into a negative thought cycle does nothing to alter the situation; in fact, all it can do is make matters worse.

Assessing a situation without adding self-judgment can be hard, but it is possible. The key is finding the distinction between what you did in the situation and how you feel about what you did. Accurately finding that distinction requires **self-compassion**—that is, being realistic about what you could and could not do, given what you were up against.

> ***Self-Judgment:*** *"My coworker and I don't agree on politics. I can't help but argue with them, and I always get angry and defensive. Each time I end up feeling horrible about them and myself. I can't believe I get sucked in each time."*
>
> ***Acceptance/Self-Compassion:*** *"My coworker and I will never agree on politics. This will not change. How can I change my relationship with the stimulus to break the negative self-critical cycle? What can I do to accept this, rather than get caught up in the emotion of it? I can accept that this will occur, recognize my own involvement, and not become attached to it. Yes, I have reacted poorly in the past. And yes, I don't agree with their beliefs. But I don't need to change them—I can't anyway. I just need to accept their stance and not get pulled into the debate."*

CUT YOURSELF SOME SLACK

For some first responders, practicing self-compassion during times of stress, challenges, or pressure can be especially difficult. Given the nature of the job, they often face incidents filled with trauma, suffering, and pain, and it's their responsibility to focus their efforts on the people affected. Naturally, this results in their personal needs being put on the back burner. Even after the incident is over, they tend to downplay their own emotional state, not viewing it as an important need. It's hard to switch gears from caring for others to giving yourself the same type of care. Just as it's always the mechanic whose car is never fixed and the cobbler who has no shoes, the tendency of first responders is to reserve their remarkable abilities of presence, calm, and care for the people they serve, while pushing themselves to "just get over it."

But compassion is not just for people who have directly experienced extreme tragedy or are in the middle of an emergency. Furthermore, offering yourself compassion does not mean you are broken and need to be fixed. It just means giving yourself a break, being kind and understanding toward yourself, rather than throwing yourself under the bus for all the things you didn't or couldn't do. It's very similar to the recognition and redirection principle we discussed in chapter 8. Acceptance asks us to recognize what happened and that it cannot be changed, while self-compassion asks us to focus on what we can learn from the experience, including what went right along with what went wrong, and let go of our personal attachment to the outcome.

For Joan's experience, this would mean:

- **Accepting Unchangeable External Factors:** The boy broke his neck on the initial impact. The water was extremely rough and made it extra hard to swim in while keeping him alive.
- **Focus on Learning:** If the situation allows, in the future be extra cautious of neck position.
- **What Went Right Versus Wrong:** Joan saved the boy's life.
- **Letting Go:** Joan did the best that anyone could do, given the circumstances. She did her job and did it well. This was not the first or last time she saved a life. The beaches are lucky to have her guarding them. Thank you, Joan.

REPEATED EXPOSURE TO TRAGEDY

First responders have a particularly close relationship with self-judgment through their repeated exposure to death, violence, and destruction. This can lead to system-wide dysregulation, ranging from diminished immune response (i.e., frequently getting sick) to more serious issues like depression, anxiety, posttraumatic stress, and even substance abuse. It can also affect their ability to form healthy relationships and even their sense of self-worth. A study that was published in *Frontiers in Behavioral Neuroscience* "suggests that the price of repeated traumatic exposure reflects a more general impairment, which may affect the way first responders interpret and react to their environment."* In other words, repeated exposure can impact a first responder's entire life, external and internal.

The rescue Joan made that day was one of many tragic on-the-job-encounters she had over the course of her employment. She spent the next 20 years blaming herself for how she had rescued the surfer, reflecting on and negatively judging her every move. As mentioned in the introduction, this is a common factor among first responders: carrying that "one tragic story," in which they didn't do enough or felt helpless against the enormity of the situation. Our brains are actually designed to do this—to focus on the worst aspects of our most traumatic experiences so that we'll do our utmost to avoid them in the future. Moreover, in my observation, the stories that "stick" tend to have a connection to the first responders' personal lives and/or past experiences. This is what makes it so critical to identify when we're locked in self-judgment and to practice acceptance and self-compassion.

The reality was that Joan responded within the constraints of her circumstances and the environment. Moreover, while the boy suffered paralysis, Joan did in fact save his life. Training the brain's awareness of self-judgment is the first step in mindfully managing the suffering we experience from outcomes we can't control.

TACTICAL BRAIN TRAINING IN ACTION

Scenario: Joan spends 20 years suffering from guilt and self-imposed judgment.

Awareness: The guilt constantly weighs heavy on her shoulders until, finally, she realizes this feeling is not healthy or self-serving.

Internal Signal: She realizes that she's constantly questioning not only her past rescues but also her life choices, and even second-guessing herself in the middle of current rescues.

Amygdala: Tragedy is everywhere. Just wait, it's going to happen again. And it will be ugly. And it will likely end in a disaster you caused, just like you did last time. In fact, every part of your life will end in a disaster you have created. So, stay on high alert—ALL THE TIME!

PFC: Let me know when to jump in, Amygdala. Just say the word.

* Levy-Gigi, E., Richter-Levin, G., & Kéri, S. (2014). The hidden price of repeated traumatic exposure: Different cognitive deficits in different first-responders. *Frontiers in Behavioral Neuroscience, 8*, 281. https://doi.org/10.3389/fnbeh.2014.00281

Mindfulness in Action:

- Awareness: *I feel like I am tense all the time, waiting for the other shoe to drop, when I will inevitably screw up again.*
- Paying attention: *I should intentionally look at how I feel when the thoughts of guilt and self-doubt come to mind.*
- Present moment: *These moments of cyclical thinking are connected to feelings of blame. When this happens, I notice that I no longer stand tall, my head lowers, my eyes cast down, and I feel like I'm walking through quicksand.*
- Non-judgmentally: *This is* how *I feel in this moment, not* who *I am as a person.*

Mindfulness Intervention: *I should practice* ***Non-Judgmental Awareness****. I am feeling sluggish and hyperfocused on doubting myself. I should look at the situation for what it was and not make it worse by adding additional suffering. The pain from that rescue 20 years ago still exists, but self-doubt and guilt are only making an unfortunate situation worse. I should reframe my thinking from* I am to blame for the incident *to* This incident was bad. *When my thoughts turn to* I *or* my, *I can change it to* the situation. *Instead of* Whatever is about to happen will be my fault, *I can change the thought to* This is the situation—now what can be done?

Amygdala: Looks like there isn't a tragedy about to occur. Just everyday life. PFC, direct us on what to do.

PFC: Take the situation for whatever it is. No self-blame needed. One foot in front of the other.

WALKING THE WALK . . .

I lost 90 percent of this chapter while I was writing it. I was on a Zoom call, something happened that caused my entire computer to shut down, and poof! Chapter 10 was gone. It seems that somehow my word processing program's AutoSave got turned off. And guess what I did? I completely blamed myself for being a dumbass. How could I have neglected to manually save my work as I was writing? What a rookie move!

> *For two full days, my mind kept spinning with "if-onlys": If only I was using Google Docs instead of Microsoft Word. . . . If only I'd made an outline of this chapter, like I did for the others. . . . If only I was smarter and could remember what I previously wrote. . . . I got so caught up in criticizing myself that I was unable to focus on my work. The more time I lost, the more at fault I felt. Then it hit me: I couldn't focus on writing because I was stuck in self-judgment.*
>
> *. . . And then I remembered what I'd been writing about!*
>
> *I literally fell on the floor laughing. When I got up, I remembered what I was supposed to do in these situations. Time to practice what I preached: The computer shut down. My document was not saved. It happened. I can't do anything about the past, only how I interact with the future. I am not annoying. The situation is annoying.*
>
> *These acceptance-oriented thoughts helped calm my nervous system, dissipating the stress so that my thinking came back online. And a strange thing occurred. I am convinced the rewritten chapter is better than the original one I wrote. So, yay me! Also, I now constantly save my document, even with AutoSave back on.*

PRACTICING MINDFULNESS

Mindfulness teaches us to look at how we react to a situation, not just in the moment that it occurs but also when we look back at our involvement (or lack thereof) in it. Mindfulness helps us distinguish between **inevitable suffering** and **optional suffering**, cultivating our ability to direct compassion toward ourselves:

- **Inevitable suffering:** The original suffering from the incident is unchangeable
- **Optional suffering:** The feelings of self-judgment associated with the incident, which can be changed through acceptance and self-compassion

There's an old parable that helps us understand these two types of suffering. The story goes that someone is walking through the woods and is suddenly shot by an arrow that missed its mark. No doubt about it, this first arrow causes suffering; both the injury and the pain it brings are out of the person's control. But if the person begins to reproach themselves for "letting" it happen (*What was I thinking, walking through the woods at this hour? Why wasn't I paying more attention to my surroundings? Maybe I deserve this—why am I always screwing up?*), that suffering is considered the second arrow. Unlike the first arrow, the second arrow is elective; it results from the person's attachment to the outcome of the first arrow.

Mindfulness helps us decrease suffering from the second arrow by managing how we see ourselves connected to any given situation. This can be accomplished by incorporating the concept of **non-judgmental awareness**—that is, observing your actions without personal judgment or emotional entanglement. One way to incorporate non-judgmental awareness is by changing the way you verbalize a feeling. Strange as it sounds, this simple shift can change the way you think about a situation. For example, instead of saying to yourself *I am upset* or *I am sad*, you change the wording to *This is upsetting* or *This is sadness*. This reframe allows for the idea that our feelings don't define who we are. You are not sadness. You are not pain. Framing the thought as *This situation is painful* implies that once the situation changes, the pain may decrease. This type of rephrasing helps us move away from falling into the self-judgment cycle.

There will always be people and situations that cause us physical pain and emotional discomfort. By practicing non-judgmental awareness, you become better equipped to separate the inevitable suffering from the optional suffering. This concept holds even more significance for first responders, who are consistently presented with situations where negative outcomes are a reality. Cultivating non-judgmental awareness is critical to decrease our vulnerability to the second arrow.

Through repeated practice of non-judgmental awareness, Joan was eventually able to reframe her thoughts about that awful day 20 years ago. Instead of questioning her every move and blaming herself for the outcome, she was able to accept the situation for what it was: a tragic accident, the first arrow. The voice inside her head that told her she was to blame for what had happened started to shift. Instead of thinking and saying things like "I am sad about the outcome of the situation" or "I feel guilty for how I handled things," she now repeats things like "The situation was bad" and "The outcome of the situation was sad." It may seem like a small change, but the difference it made is immense. Joan as a person is not defined by the suffering of that one beach rescue. She is a mother, an employee, a sister, a friend, and so much more. All these different parts of her life factor into her identity and value.

CONTEMPLATION QUESTIONS

Have you ever suffered from regret? *If only . . . , If I could have . . . ,* or *I should have . . .*

What do you currently feel about the regret?

DON'T FORGET!

Fill out the first column of the self-assessment chart before practicing the mindfulness intervention.

Mindfulness Intervention Self-Assessment

NON-JUDGMENTAL AWARENESS

The self-assessment chart that follows is designed to track your progress. This chart will help you assess three things:

- How you feel before doing the mindfulness intervention, from 1 = you feel your best to 5 = you feel your worst
- How you feel after doing the mindfulness intervention, from 1 = you feel your best to 5 = you feel your worst
- How you felt while practicing the mindfulness intervention, from 1 = it was pleasant to 5 = it was unpleasant

Fill out the first column of the chart *before* you move on to the mindfulness intervention practice in this chapter. *After* you've practiced the intervention, fill out the second and third columns.

Remember that these assessments are subjective. There are no right or wrong answers and no judgment. And make it easy on yourself—write it down directly in the book, and you can always come back to it for reference.

MINDFULNESS INTERVENTION SELF-ASSESSMENT

Pre-assessment	Post-assessment	Summary Assessment
Overall Mood/Quality (1 = Best → 5 = Worst)	Overall Mood/Quality (1 = Best → 5 = Worst)	Quality of Intervention (1 = Pleasant → 5 = Unpleasant)

Mindfulness Intervention

NON-JUDGMENTAL AWARENESS

This practice teaches the brain to notice self-judgment and then replace it with nonattachment and self-compassion. By reframing thoughts and taking the *self* out of the equation, the brain learns to let go of self-judgment and instead focus on the situation at hand, and what can be done within the current circumstance.

How to Practice

Set a timer for practicing or do what feels comfortable for you.

1. **Find a comfortable position.** Either sit in a way that is comfortable or stand against a wall. You should have a feeling of sitting or standing tall, in a way that creates a sense of being aware of your surroundings. Allow your eyes to close or keep them open and focused on a single point in front of you.
2. **Choose an anchor.** Begin by choosing an anchor: breathing, listening, sensing, square breathing. Settle into a comfortable pattern for a few rounds.
3. **Tune into awareness.** As you focus on your anchor, you will notice that your mind wanders to stories or random thoughts. Every time you have a thought or image or story, rather than judge yourself for not being able to focus on your anchor, simply say to yourself *Thought* or *Image* or *Story* and return to the anchor.
4. **Rephrase to nonattachment.** Rather than connect yourself to feelings of judgment and stress, redirect thoughts and make them general, taking yourself out of the equation. For example, notice each time you think *I did it again* or *I am irritated* or *I can't believe I can't do this for longer than a second*, then rephrase those thoughts to *It happened* or *This is irritation* or *This is frustration*, taking yourself out of the equation.

5. **Self-compassion.** Focus on your anchor, notice your mind wandering, phrase your thinking in a non-judgmental way, and then congratulate yourself for noticing and reframing away from self-judgment. You can even think *Great job noticing that I was being judgmental!* Repeat the cycle for as long as you would like to practice.
6. **Three closing breaths.** Once you have practiced for a comfortable amount of time, take three deep closing breaths, exhaling longer than inhaling. Bring your attention to your feet on the ground and think about what they feel like. Take one more breath and open your eyes, or just refocus on the room.

Mindfulness Intervention QR Code: Guided Non-Judgmental Awareness

You can check out a recorded guided practice here:

Mindfulness Intervention Self-Assessment

Return to the self-assessment chart to fill out the postassessment and summary assessment columns *after* you practice the mindfulness intervention.

CHAPTER 11

RESILIENCE

"Exploring the unknown requires
tolerating uncertainty."

– Brian Greene

In this chapter, I will address:

- Gina's story of disconnecting during a moment of chaos
- Resilience
- How mindfulness helps us bounce back from stress and trauma
- Mindfulness intervention: **Grounding—Three Breaths**

TRYING TO REMEMBER

Yes, this chapter is about me. I had just dropped my 12-year-old daughter at soccer practice. The route home took me down a very narrow street, leaving my F150 truck with no room for error. I also had my nine-pound Morkie dog, Pippin, in the car. While I was stopped in traffic, I noticed three people sitting on a stoop: a woman sitting in between two men who were connected to her in a strange way. My spidey sense went off—something was wrong. My first thought was sexual assault because of the way they were holding her. Feeling protective, I rolled down the passenger window, looked them all in the eyes, and casually but firmly asked if everything was okay. At that exact moment, the woman's head fell to her chest and her entire body slumped forward. Both men looked at me with fear in their eyes and shouted, "*Help!*"

At that moment, the light turned green. The cars behind me were honking, barely able to pass my big truck, and my yippy dog was getting agitated. Waving at the traffic to pass me, I called 911 and informed the operator what I'd seen—to me, it looked like an overdose situation.

The 911 responder asked if the woman was breathing. I said I didn't know.

"Can you find out?"

All cool and collected, I responded, "Sure, why not?" and yelled the same question out my window to the men on the stoop. One of them shouted back, "I don't think so!"

Still super chill, I reported his answer back to the 911 responder, trying to ignore the fact that my truck was blocking traffic and my dog was having a meltdown.

Then the 911 responder said, "She needs CPR."

Yeah, I thought, *sounds like a good idea.*

After a pause, the 911 responder clarified. "*You* need to give her CPR."

I responded, "I'm on a very busy street, my truck is huge, cars really can't get by, and my dog is in the car." While I didn't specifically say it, I was sure she'd agree that I wasn't in a position to get out and help someone who was dying. Bad timing—so what's plan B?

Instead, she said, in a very stern tone (which was completely called for), "Ma'am, I need you to get out of your car and administer CPR *right now*!"

CALM BEFORE THE STORM

I realize now, looking back at this incident, that I wasn't at all "cool and collected." In fact, I was completely disconnected from the situation. I had dropped out of my window of tolerance and was now frozen in the **hypovigilant zone**.

HYPERVIGILANT ZONE	• Extremely anxious • Angry • Out of control	• Overwhelmed • Can't think • Fight or flight response
DYSREGULATED	• Begin to feel agitated • Revved up	• Don't feel comfortable
ZONE OF TOLERANCE	• Content • Best able to cope	• Calm but not tired • Alert but not anxious
DYSREGULATED	• Begin to shut down • Lose track of time	• Feel sluggish
HYPOVIGILANT ZONE	• Feel zoned out • Numb	• Desensitized • Freeze response

Also known as the freeze response, hypovigilance doesn't always look like a deer caught in the headlights. It can also look like chillin', lack of urgency, taking things in stride. When our brain is overwhelmed, sometimes disconnecting from the situation makes it easier to cope with the chaos. It's a natural subconscious reaction that can feel protective, providing a false sense of calm and control that definitely feels better than the uncertainty and urgency we're confronting. My seeming lack of concern for the tragedy unfolding in front of me came from my brain trying to create safety for me. But when the 911 responder sternly jarred me out of my freeze state, I saw the need to push through my hypovigilance. I answered, "Yes ma'am," left my barking dog behind in the truck, and went to assess the situation.

SUCK IT UP

The ability to push through hardships can be motivated by pride, strength, or necessity, or it can be motivated by guilt, shame, or stigma. Pushing through can sometimes look like sucking it up to do what needs to be done. In fact, "suck it up" is not an uncommon thing to say and hear in sports, family, work, and life. However, this phrase carries the weight of being controlled by an outside source of suffering. It is, in its own way, an FFFF reaction.

At the other end of the "push through" spectrum is **resilience**. While "sucking it up" implies doing something against your desire or your will, resilience implies a conscious, freely made choice in the matter. In his book *The Body Keeps the Score*, Dr. Bessel van der Kolk writes, "Resilience is the product of agency: knowing that what you do can make a difference."* This element of choice is connected to feelings of positivity regarding the outcome, even if the outcome does not turn out the way you had hoped or intended.

IMPLICATIONS OF SUCK IT UP

- Unquestioned acceptance of a situation
- Not allowed to complain
- Dismissive feelings
- Necessity to just *move on*
- No questions asked
- Lack of choice
- Guilt
- Shame

IMPLICATIONS OF RESILIENCE

- Ability to pivot
- Coping skills to handle difficult experiences
- Recovery from challenges
- Perseverance in the face of adversity
- Ability to adjust
- Agency, or free will, to make choices
- Strength to persevere
- Control over decisions
- Ability to make a difference
- Positive association with outcome

* van der Kolk, B. (2014). *The body keeps the score: Brain, mind, and body in the healing of trauma*. Viking.

BOUNCING BACK

Resilience is the ability to learn from mistakes and find solutions to problems, rather than getting stuck in thoughts of failure. Resilience helps us keep momentum in the face of adversity. It's about embracing the challenge, hitting things head on, and when the situation hits back, getting back up again, and again, and again. Best of all, resilience is a skill that can be trained.

> *It's worth noting that there are numerous situations where you should stay down rather than push through. Let's say you broke your leg during a marathon—not a good time to push through! Resilience does not mean hurting yourself in order to look strong. That would be "suck it up."*

When I was a kid, my parents bought me a "bozo" punching bag, the kind with the clown face on the front and the heavy sand in the bottom that bounces back after every hit. I had some pent-up anger issues, and rather than smash my fists into walls (like my father often did), they thought I'd be better off taking out my anger on the bozo bag.

If you have ever hit one of these bags, you may recall the feeling of hitting it really hard, only to have it bounce right back at you, ready for another blow. The harder you hit the bag, the harder it goes down, and the longer it takes to recover and balance itself. It's a good analogy for getting knocked down in life. Think of the mind as the bozo bag and emotions as punches. When hit with a small emotion, the mind may momentarily lose balance, becoming distracted or caught up in negative thoughts, but if you keep your wits about you, you can shake off the blow and recover your focus pretty quickly. But when hit with a strong emotion, it's a lot easier to get knocked down. The bigger the emotion, the harder the fall, and the more difficult it is to get back up and find your mental balance again. But TBT helps us develop the ability and confidence to create a strategy for getting back up.

THE 5, 4, 3, 2, 1 EXERCISE

Here's a little "bonus" exercise for those moments when you get mentally knocked down and can't seem to steady yourself. When that happens, stop where you are and identify:

- Five things you see
- Four things you feel
- Three things you hear
- Two things you smell
- One thing you taste

This exercise assists in stabilizing and calming the nervous system when it "hits the ground," helping it recover and bringing the rational brain back online. By focusing on something external, the internal mind has a chance to calm down, letting go of the emotion and reengaging with the thinking mind. It can then refocus without the attached emotional baggage.

THE PUNCHES KEPT COMING

Being asked to try resuscitating someone was a hard first punch to my mental balance. Feeling forced into a situation I was not prepared for, I got out of my truck and confirmed that the woman was not breathing and there was no heartbeat. But when it came time to actually perform CPR, I froze once again. The 911 responder was telling me what to do, but the words sounded mumbled. A crowd was gathering around us. I remember looking over at Pippin in the truck window as cars piled up behind. I could not think, I could not act; I just stood there. Realizing this woman's life was literally in my hands felt like the knockout punch; I mentally hit the ground hard.

Then something kicked in, like a distant voice saying, *You are out of your window of tolerance. This is the moment you have spent years training for. Now's the time. Find your way back to tolerable.* Here is where I made the pivot from feeling forced into a situation to finding resilience and bouncing back.

TACTICAL BRAIN TRAINING IN ACTION

Scenario: Gina is trying to help a woman suffering from cardiac arrest.

Awareness: Gina realizes she is dealing with a challenging situation and is letting it get the better of her.

Internal Signal: She is suffering from a lack of feelings (i.e., she is unattached to the situation).

Amygdala: This is bad. We've seen a lot, but not like this. If you just stand here, maybe it will all work itself out. That way you don't have to try to resuscitate her, possibly encountering failure. The worst kind of failure: loss of life.

PFC: Something is going on, but Amygdala jumped in and took over, so I'm just going to hang out here.

Mindfulness in Action:

- Awareness: *My reaction is not commensurate with the situation. I am checked out. I should be taking action right now.*
- Paying attention: *I need to check in and do an assessment of my body and mind.*
- Present moment: *My casual approach to this tragedy is showing up as an emotional wall between me and this incident. I feel no connection to her or what she is experiencing. I am numb and disconnected.*
- Non-judgmentally: *I hit the ground, yes. But I can still bounce back. A setback is not failure. Great job noticing what was going on!*

Mindfulness Intervention: *What can I do right now to get my mind back to thinking? I need to find and feel a connection. Maybe if I focus on my feet on the ground, I can begin to connect to my body, which will help create a connection to my thoughts. I will take three breaths while focusing on grounding.*

Amygdala: This is still an emergency, but it's one we can handle. Time to bounce back. PFC, do the CPR thing.

PFC: Step 1, check for breathing and heartbeat. Negative to both. Step 2, start compressions.

I am happy to say that once my brain started working, I was able to get my act together. I remember actually saying out loud, "This is the moment." I stood tall, told everyone around me to be quiet (I may have said "*Shut up!*"—there was so much yelling!), took a wide stance, and brought my attention to the feeling of my feet on the pavement. It felt solid, stable, and grounding. I took three breaths in that position, then got to work.

As I'd been taught in my CPR training, I began singing the song "Stayin' Alive" in my mind and coordinating my chest compressions with the song's rhythm. After only about 20 compressions (which felt like forever), I was able to revive the woman. Then her heart stopped again. Luckily, that was when the paramedics showed up. They gave her Narcan, she started breathing, and they loaded her up in the ambulance. At that point, I literally ran back to Pippin and my truck. (If this sounds to you like a flight reaction, you're catching on quick!)

PRACTICING MINDFULNESS

Just like with training for a marathon, rehearsing for a presentation, or studying for an exam, resilience requires practice. As with other mindfulness qualities we've learned about, practicing resilience helps create neural connections between being mentally knocked down and getting back up, building a mindset that it's possible to make a mistake and still recover. In fact, resilience is baked into every type of mindfulness intervention in this book. Practicing multiple interventions not only decreases the time it takes to choose one that will work for a given situation but also helps decrease the recovery time between popping out of your window of tolerance and regaining emotional balance—the amount of time you spend stressing out decreases and is replaced with organizing strategies for emotional balance. Even with practice, you will still hit edges and still get knocked down, and you may even go down hard. But the practice helps your mind acknowledge and remember that it can recover.

CONTEMPLATION QUESTIONS

What does it mean to be resilient?

____

____

____

____

Do you have an example of when you were able to bounce back?

____

____

____

____

DON'T FORGET!

Fill out the first column of the self-assessment chart before practicing the mindfulness intervention.

Mindfulness Intervention Self-Assessment

GROUNDING—THREE BREATHS

The self-assessment chart that follows is designed to track your progress. This chart will help you assess three things:

- How you feel before doing the mindfulness intervention, from 1 = you feel your best to 5 = you feel your worst
- How you feel after doing the mindfulness intervention, from 1 = you feel your best to 5 = you feel your worst
- How you felt while practicing the mindfulness intervention, from 1 = it was pleasant to 5 = it was unpleasant

Fill out the first column of the chart *before* you move on to the mindfulness intervention practice in this chapter. *After* you've practiced the intervention, fill out the second and third columns.

Remember that these assessments are subjective. There are no right or wrong answers and no judgment. And make it easy on yourself—write it down directly in the book, and you can always come back to it for reference.

MINDFULNESS INTERVENTION SELF-ASSESSMENT

Pre-assessment	Post-assessment	Summary Assessment
Overall Mood/Quality (1 = Best → 5 = Worst)	Overall Mood/Quality (1 = Best → 5 = Worst)	Quality of Intervention (1 = Pleasant → 5 = Unpleasant)

Mindfulness Intervention

GROUNDING—THREE BREATHS

This practice can be incorporated into daily life. It can be done during downtime, and even during high-stress situations. It trains for present-moment awareness, which has the secondary benefit of calming the nervous system. Training with this mindfulness intervention teaches the brain to go from a stressed state to a calm state by tuning into or paying attention to a sensation, then connecting it to a longer slow exhale.

How to Practice

Set a timer for practicing or do what feels comfortable for you.

1. **Begin wherever you are.** You can stand, sit, drive, walk, or lie down.
2. **Breath 1.** Inhale through your nose, halfway filling your lungs. Then inhale, fully inflating your lungs, and focus on listening to the sounds in your environment. Exhale out your mouth for a count of six (or longer).
3. **Breath 2.** Inhale through your nose, halfway filling your lungs. Then inhale, fully inflating your lungs, and bring your attention to something you can feel. Your seat in the chair, your hands on the steering wheel, your feet on the ground. Feel the points of contact with you and the object. Exhale out your mouth for a count of six (or longer).
4. **Breath 3.** Inhale through your nose, halfway filling your lungs. Then inhale, fully inflating your lungs, and think about where you feel your breath: in your nose, in your belly, in your chest. Exhale out your mouth for a count of six (or longer), and relax associated muscles. Soften face, relax belly, soften chest muscles.

Mindfulness Intervention QR Code: Guided Grounding—Three Breaths

You can check out a recorded guided practice here:

Mindfulness Intervention Self-Assessment

Return to the self-assessment chart to fill out the postassessment and summary assessment columns *after* you practice the mindfulness intervention.

CHAPTER 12

BURNOUT

"Your reward will be the widening of the horizon as you climb. And if you achieve that reward you will ask no other."

– Cecilia Payne-Gaposchkin

In this chapter, I will address:

- Isaac's story of experiencing a mental crash after four years on the job
- Burnout
- How mindfulness helps build the muscle of noticing what is occurring internally
- Mindfulness intervention: **Somatic Embodiment**

IT WAS ALL FINE, AND THEN . . .

I received a call from a paramedic named Isaac who was asking for advice on how to work with a sudden onset of burnout. He said he felt confused because, until recently, he had experienced nothing but excitement about his job. Even with all the trauma he had seen, he'd never noticed any negative mental effects for himself. But now, out of the blue, his on-the-job experiences seemed to be taking a mental toll, and his emotions felt like they were boiling over.

This was extra bewildering for Isaac because this job was everything he had ever wanted. After trying a few different careers throughout his 20s—desk work, retail counter, personal trainer—he'd realized that what he really wanted was a job with more excitement, higher energy, and the potential to make a difference. Isaac explained that he had always thrived on physical activity and loved change. He grew up playing competitive sports and continued to during college, and from the second he could ride, he had raced his motorcycle through the countryside.

At the age of 28, Isaac became a paramedic, and from the first day, the high stress and fast pace of work kept him engaged. The freedom and rush of adrenaline felt like home; as he explained it, he was "made to be a paramedic," and his intention had always been to stick with this career until retirement. Up until a few months before our call, he had never felt particularly tied to any of the tragedies he had encountered. But recently, he'd been experiencing panic attacks in connection with work, specifically to the trauma he had witnessed over the last four years. He had three main questions for me:

- "Why have things gone so well for four years, and only now I'm experiencing a lack of motivation to continue?"
- "How can I find my way back to loving my job?"
- "Can mindfulness help me have sympathy for victims, while not becoming attached and possibly traumatized?"

We started by talking about what an average workday looked like for him. He explained that from the second he arrived at work to the very end of his shift, his focus was purely on procedure and patient care. At the beginning of his career, as soon as a call came over the radio, he would run through a mental checklist, going over all his medical training. If it was a car accident, he imagined scenarios and resulting treatment. If it was an assault, he would think of things to say to the victim that might be calming. If it was cardiac arrest, he would imagine himself doing CPR. (Hopefully better than I did with the woman suffering an overdose!) En route to the scene, his mind was filled with possibilities and outcomes; when he arrived, his brain would move into action. There was always something new, something he hadn't considered previously, and he continually pulled from his knowledge base, readjusting to take the current scenario into consideration. This entire process was what Isaac thrived on—the constant challenge of being in the moment, assessing what was possible, and pivoting until he saw results.

With four years under his belt, however, he had reached a point where he no longer felt the need to play out every step beforehand. Even though every call was still different, Isaac explained that each call now appeared as a variation of all the previous experiences he'd had. While he still envisioned each incident en route, the space in his mind that would normally go through a checklist of procedures was now left idle. Instead of thinking about how to do something, he instead focused on the victims themselves and their personal outcomes. The job no longer felt exciting to him. Rather, he felt overwhelmed by the pain and suffering he was seeing.

STAY THE COURSE

Isaac's trajectory over the last four years—from connection with the excitement of his job to hyper-focus on all the human suffering he had witnessed—is totally normal. Sometimes the mind is so occupied with *doing* that it doesn't really feel anything in moments of distress. This is one of the brain's more impressive techniques for keeping our focus on a task. If the mind were to immediately go into an emotional reaction in an emergent situation, those involved in rescue, protection, or treatment tasks would not be very effective at their job. So congrats to our brains for being able to disconnect so they can get the job done!

However, this power to disconnect in the moment of doing is just a delay of the inevitable emotional reaction. This was the case for Isaac. After four years of unconsciously guarding himself from becoming too emotionally connected, the buildup of witnessing the suffering resulted in overempathizing with the patients and victims. His mind had finally reached its threshold and was cracking under the physical and emotional stress. In other words, Isaac was experiencing burnout.

BURNOUT

Burnout can come on at any time during a career. For first responders, the job's high level of physical and mental stress makes burnout a constant possibility, whether they're at the end of a lifetime of service, just getting started in their career, or like Isaac, somewhere in the middle. In addition, burnout looks different for everyone. It can show up as exhaustion or as a lack of motivation. It may feel like decreased energy for everyday tasks like washing dishes or sorting through the mail, or it may feel like a sudden change of heart about your work, sometimes to the point of wanting to leave your job altogether. It may also bring a variety of other emotions, including (but not limited to):

- Fatigue
- Lack of emotion
- Sense of apathy
- Rumination
- Physical exhaustion
- Negative self-talk
- Irritability
- Lack of focus
- Depression
- Overthinking

Each of these emotions as a one-off can be challenging to manage, let alone dealing with multiple feelings at a time (which is more typical in burnout). While it can be hard to put these feelings into words, doing so can help us identify what is occurring and find lifestyle solutions like taking breaks, finding better work-life balance, incorporating healthy eating and daily exercise, and setting boundaries—all proven strategies for allaying burnout.

Of course, it's easy to look back and assess a situation after you have all the facts. It's more difficult when you are in the middle of a shitstorm to realize that you are circling the drain. This elusive link between burnout and recovery comes in the form of awareness.

THINKING TOO MUCH

In his book *Mindsight*, Dr. Daniel Siegel explains that the human brain has evolved to allow us to think about thinking. The positive side of this superpower is that it enables insight and executive functioning. Thinking deeply about our thoughts can empower us with a vivid imagination, creative problem-solving, and strong decision-making. The downside, he writes, "is that at times these new capacities allow us to think too much."* As we discussed in chapter 8, this is how we find ourselves engaged in negative rumination, critical self-talk, vivid images of doom and gloom, depression, anxiety, and poor self-image. Left unchecked, this slippery slope of negative overthinking is a breeding ground for burnout.

As we've seen, TBT trains the mind to look at a thought, identify it, then redirect it to something helpful rather than harmful. With burnout specifically, this redirection should be focused on a positive outcome or at least the possibilities for one, even if it's just the reward of *not* feeling negative about something.

Without the possibility of reward or success, continuing a task can seem pointless. I once worked with a member of a search and rescue unit who explained this dynamic in the context of training rescue dogs. These dogs were deployed to locate survivors following a significant earthquake, but there were times when no survivors were found. To sustain the dogs' motivation for continuing the search, handlers would orchestrate scenarios where a team member would hide, and the dogs were tasked to "discover" them. By ensuring these orchestrated scenarios were successful, the handlers provided the dogs with positive reinforcement that encouraged their commitment to the search for the real earthquake survivors.

Training the brain to think in positive or helpful terms, especially with a "reward" attached, creates or reinforces the brain's desire to continue. Instead of ruminating or judging ourselves for our lack of success, we can use our power of thinking about thinking to reframe our thoughts in terms of opportunities. Training to think about our thoughts from a **learner** perspective versus a **judger** perspective can help decrease the feelings of mental and emotional drain. Training the mind to see the possibility of new possibilities can be all it takes to revive our motivation and mitigate burnout.

TRAIN TO FEEL NEGATIVITY

The feelings of burnout, such as overwhelm and negativity, are typically connected to a felt sensation in the body. For example, if you think about a past argument with a partner or friend and really pay attention to your body, you can probably feel agitation and discomfort. Maybe you get prickly skin or a tight neck; maybe you feel like you need to get up and move, or just make some adjustments while you are

* Siegel, D. J. (2010). *Mindsight: The new science of personal transformation*. Bantam Books.

sitting. By training to notice what "unease" feels like, you begin to build connections in the mind between a specific type of negative thought and how it feels in your body. Over time, you begin to notice a physical shift in the moment when the negativity is occurring. Training for this type of present-moment awareness triggers the brain to notice the judger, then reminds the mind to become the learner. As the learner, you're more inclined to look at a situation in an uplifting way, which reinforces positive behavior and decreases the desire to go down the negative (and exhausting) path of self-judgment. The more you repeat this shift from feelings of burnout to thoughts of learning, the more control you have over your well-being and the situation.

Judger	vs.	Learner
What's wrong?		What works?
Who's to blame?		What am I responsible for?
How can I prove I'm right?		What are the facts?
How can I be in control?		What are my choices?
How could I get hurt?		What can I learn?
Why bother?	?	What's possible?

TACTICAL BRAIN TRAINING IN ACTION

Scenario: Isaac is feeling a disconnect with work but is worried that if he tries for deeper engagement with his patients, he will become overwhelmed with emotional connection.

Awareness: Isaac knows something needs to change.

Internal Signal: He is overthinking, feeling anxious, and at the same time, unmotivated.

Amygdala: Time to ditch this whole paramedic thing. Run and take cover from all others who are suffering. Career #4, here we come.

PFC: I'm on board with that. I can draft a new job goal.

Mindfulness in Action:

- Awareness: *I have only been working as a paramedic for four years, yet I feel the weight of a lifetime of suffering.*
- Paying attention: *Now is a good time to address this feeling.*
- Present moment: *I feel that my excitement for the job has dulled. I am distancing myself and focusing on the negative.*
- Non-judgmentally: *It's okay to disconnect a little, so as not to spiral. Glad I noticed when I did!*

Mindfulness Intervention: *I should try something that brings awareness to my body so that during these times of disconnect, I can feel it and find a way back to the present moment. Rather than thinking about all the negative, I will think about what is occurring in my body as a path to decreasing feelings of burnout. I think I should try the Somatic Embodiment intervention.*

Amygdala: The highway is cleared for the transformation of information.

PFC: Let's check in with the body by practicing Somatic Embodiment. Notice the length of my body and connect with a feeling of strength. Notice the width of my body and connect with protection and boundaries. Notice the front of my body and note the endless potential of what is ahead of me. Rather than judge what is occurring, learn about what is possible.

Isaac reported that after just three weeks of practicing the **Somatic Embodiment** intervention, he was noticing a decrease in his anxiety and once again finding joy in his job. He would still think about the accidents and trauma he was about to encounter, but now he looked at these situations from a learner's perspective, asking himself questions about what was coming up for him, both physically and mentally. This does not mean that his emotions disappeared, or that he never felt stressed. It does mean that when emotions and stress arose, he was able to notice the feelings and manage them.

PRACTICING MINDFULNESS

For a first responder, mindfulness is key to sustaining empathy for patients, victims, and others adversely affected in the community, while not becoming emotionally attached and possibly traumatized. It teaches us to identify and process our thoughts so as not to be overcome with the emotion, and at the same time connect with what is occurring in the body to allow for a learner approach. Practicing mindfulness solidifies the connections between the body and the mind, enabling easier access to the way they inform each other in moments of stress. Identification of what's happening in the mind and body takes our thinking out of the "spin cycle" by disengaging it from our emotions and directing it to a felt sense/body sensation. This calms the nervous system and brings executive thinking back online. Repeated training through practice of the mindfulness interventions helps establish a pattern of positive thinking that fights the onset of burnout, enabling meaningful connections with work and people in an empowering way.

CONTEMPLATION QUESTIONS

Have you experienced feelings of burnout? How would you describe those feelings?

____

____

____

____

Was there an incident that occurred where you felt detached at the time, only to think about it later with a strong emotion?

____

____

____

____

DON'T FORGET!

Fill out the first column of the self-assessment chart before practicing the mindfulness intervention.

Mindfulness Intervention Self-Assessment

SOMATIC EMBODIMENT

The self-assessment chart that follows is designed to track your progress. This chart will help you assess three things:

- How you feel before doing the mindfulness intervention, from 1 = you feel your best to 5 = you feel your worst
- How you feel after doing the mindfulness intervention, from 1 = you feel your best to 5 = you feel your worst
- How you felt while practicing the mindfulness intervention, from 1 = it was pleasant to 5 = it was unpleasant

Fill out the first column of the chart *before* you move on to the mindfulness intervention practice in this chapter. *After* you've practiced the intervention, fill out the second and third columns.

Remember that these assessments are subjective. There are no right or wrong answers and no judgment. And make it easy on yourself—write it down directly in the book, and you can always come back to it for reference.

MINDFULNESS INTERVENTION SELF-ASSESSMENT

Pre-assessment	Post-assessment	Summary Assessment
Overall Mood/Quality (1 = Best → 5 = Worst)	Overall Mood/Quality (1 = Best → 5 = Worst)	Quality of Intervention (1 = Pleasant → 5 = Unpleasant)

Mindfulness Intervention

SOMATIC EMBODIMENT

This practice trains us to connect the mind and body with regenerative concepts such as pride, present-moment awareness, community, past and future thinking, and gratitude. It encourages a connection with self and with those around you, while at the same time feeling a sense of boundaries. It builds a foundation for a felt sense of love, kindness, and gratitude for both others and the self.

How to Practice

Set a timer for practicing or do what feels comfortable for you.

1. **Begin by choosing a posture that's comfortable for you.** This intervention is best done standing, but you can also practice by sitting or lying down. Allow your gaze to be soft. Take a nice big inhale, and then exhale slowly.
2. **Length of body—pride/strength.** Notice the length and strength of your body. Whatever position you are in, bring attention to your feet, and continue all the way up to the top of your head. Bring to mind this idea of length, and also think about the idea of feeling strength and pride. Feel yourself standing tall or lengthening long, and connect with the sensation of your feet all the way up to the top of your head, so the entire length of your body is connected with the idea of strength and pride and length.
3. **Back of body—past.** Change your awareness to the back of the body. See if you can imagine what the back of your body looks like—the back of your head, your back, your seat, the back of your heels. Feel the space between your shirt and your back, or between your shoulder blades. Begin to connect the back body with past events. Imagine that everything that's behind you, your entire past, is connected with the backs of your shoulder blades, the back of your head, the back of your legs. Your entire back body is connected to past events.

4. **Side body—community/boundaries.** Next, move your thinking to the sides of your body, connecting with ideas of both boundaries and shared community. Bring your attention to the sides of your body, from shoulder to shoulder, hip to hip, the outer edges of your feet, maybe even ear to ear. Now imagine that these parts of your body are connecting with the outside world.

   Create a circle with your arms, circling around yourself. Connect the idea of the sides of your body and the circle of your arms with the feeling of protection and safe boundaries. Feel a connection with those around you, while also feeling protected and secure.

   Now reach your arms wide, thinking about reaching out to those in the community. Take a moment to continue connecting with the community by sending thoughts of kindness and gratitude to others. Bring to mind someone or something (maybe a pet) who you have an uncomplicated relationship with, who you feel safe with. As you bring to mind this being who creates safety, silently send these words to them: May you feel love and kindness. May you feel safe and secure. May you feel healthy and strong.

   Broaden those thoughts of loving-kindness to your inner circle or your local community or neighborhood. Bringing to mind your community, imagining all those people, send thoughts of love and gratitude: May you feel love and kindness. May you feel safe and secure.

   Feel your arms widen even more, as you move on to sending well-wishes on a larger scale, to your nation, to the world. Imagine all the people and beings on your continent, and then even further out, in the entire world: May you all feel love and kindness. May everyone, every being, every animal feel safe and secure. May you all feel healthy and strong.

   Moving from broad thinking, slowly making that circle of thoughts smaller and smaller, you can come back to your neighborhood, your community, all the way back to thinking about that first person or animal who makes you feel safe and secure. Placing your arms at your sides, connect once more with the sides of your body, the sides of your feet, your hips, your shoulders.

5. **Internal body—present moment.** Now change your awareness to focus on your internal world. Connect the idea of the internal body with present-moment awareness. What's occurring inside your body? Get curious about your heartbeat, your stomach digestion, your lungs as you inhale and exhale, your stomach as it rises and falls. Connect the internal body with the idea of what's occurring right now, in this moment. Your breath. Your heartbeat. Your digestion. Connect this awareness with all that you are, turning in to yourself. And just as you did with community, now turn thoughts of gratitude, love, and kindness inward. Think to yourself as you're standing here in this present moment: May I feel love and kindness. May I feel safe and secure. May I be healthy and strong. May I be happy.
6. **Front body—future.** Pivot to bringing awareness to the front of your body, connecting it with thoughts of future and progress. Feel your face, your chest, the front of your thighs, your toes. Think thoughts of forward movement, both physically and mentally. Think of what the future holds and all that is waiting for you; all that is behind you brought you to this moment. Feel excitement for what the future holds.
7. **Entire body—gratitude.** Finally, picture your entire body, connecting all the parts. The length of your body, the sides of your body, the back of your body, your internal body, and the front of your body. Bring it all into one thought, one image, and take a moment to send yourself some gratitude. You might say to yourself, *Great job. Great job for practicing today.* Maybe even put your hands over your heart again and say, *Thank you.*
8. **Reach up.** Now reach your arms up high, all the way over your head. Take an inhale, and as you exhale, slowly lower your arms. Just take a moment to look around and take in the colors, the sights, maybe even the sounds.
9. **Identify quality.** Get curious about what you feel. What is the quality you feel right now? And as you close this practice, give yourself one final moment of gratitude, saying to yourself once more, *Thank you. Great job.*

Mindfulness Intervention QR Code: Guided Somatic Embodiment

You can check out a recorded guided practice here:

Mindfulness Intervention Self-Assessment

Return to the self-assessment chart to fill out the postassessment and summary assessment columns *after* you practice the mindfulness intervention.

CHAPTER 13

INTUITION

"Gut instinct is the voice of the Universe within us."

– Steve Maraboli

In this chapter, I will address:

- Michael's story of listening to his intuition
- Intuition (gut instinct)
- How mindfulness helps us pick up on cues in the environment and notice the feeling of gut instinct
- Mindfulness intervention: **Sensing**

THE STOP

Michael is a police officer who likes to work the streets. Over the course of his 15-year career, he has worked various units (gangs, SWAT, criminal investigations) but ultimately always goes back on patrol. He enjoys interacting with the community and is a huge proponent of feet-on-the-ground community policing. He especially loves working with kids and leads a local Boys and Girls Club. As the club leader, he constantly walks a fine line between building trust and remaining an authoritative figure.

One day on patrol, Michael pulled over a car full of teenagers for speeding. As he approached the vehicle, he wasn't surprised to see a few faces he knew. He spoke with the driver, explaining why he pulled him over, and briefly interacted with the rest of the kids in the car to assess the general atmosphere. Michael hoped they had nothing to hide. He did not want to be unfairly suspicious, to give them a hard time, or to lose their trust, which had taken him so long to build. To his relief, it seemed clear there was no alcohol involved, at least—*Just kids being dumb*, Michael reassured himself. He gave the driver a speeding ticket and started walking back to his patrol car.

But halfway back, he noticed that something felt off. "When I was walking back," he told me later, "I felt this nagging feeling in my gut, and after 10 steps I had to turn around and go back and talk to the kids some more."

As he was walking up to the back passenger door, he glanced in the back seat, and that's when his brain made the connection between something he had seen and his strange feeling. He asked the driver to step out, placed him at the rear of the car, kept his eyes on the back seat passengers, and called for backup. He then got everyone out of the car and did a full search. After looking in every crevice of the vehicle, he found multiple illegal weapons, ammunition, and drugs. A lot of drugs.

GUT-BRAIN CONNECTION

Some first responders I talk to say that intuition exists; others say no way. More seem to agree when talking about this feeling in terms of gut instinct. This may seem like semantics to some, clarification to others. Regardless, let's stick with the term **gut instinct** for now.

Gut instinct has been described as an inner knowledge that sometimes presents as a visceral feeling. It shows up as a quick, spontaneous assessment of a situation that doesn't rely on conscious reasoning. So, what is it based on then? If thinking comes from the brain, why would we base decisions on a feeling in the gut?

In fact, studies suggest that not only is there a connection between the gut and the brain, our thoughts can also possibly originate in our stomach. One 2011 experiment looked at mice who consumed specific probiotics and found fewer visible signs of anxiety, lower levels of stress hormones, even chemical changes in the brain. In other words, when the gut is happy, the mind is relaxed and calm. The opposite is true as well: When the gut is tense, the brain feels stressed. Moreover, this stress effect continues to cycle back to the gut. When the brain feels stress, the gut feels uneasy. (Ever had a thought that makes you sick to your stomach?) In short, the gut and the brain are demonstrably intertwined, even able to "talk" to one another, which makes it pretty clear that gut instinct is real at some level.*

Not surprisingly, information processed in the gut looks a bit different from information processed in the brain. The gut can't make decisions or solve math problems, and while it does react to stress, it is unable to affect a conscious decision or action. Rather, its main ability comes in the form of releasing stress chemicals that get sent up the ladder to the brain for making decisions. It's like the gut is giving a nudge to the brain: "Hey, this sick feeling we are having means something not so great is happening—can you please figure it out?"

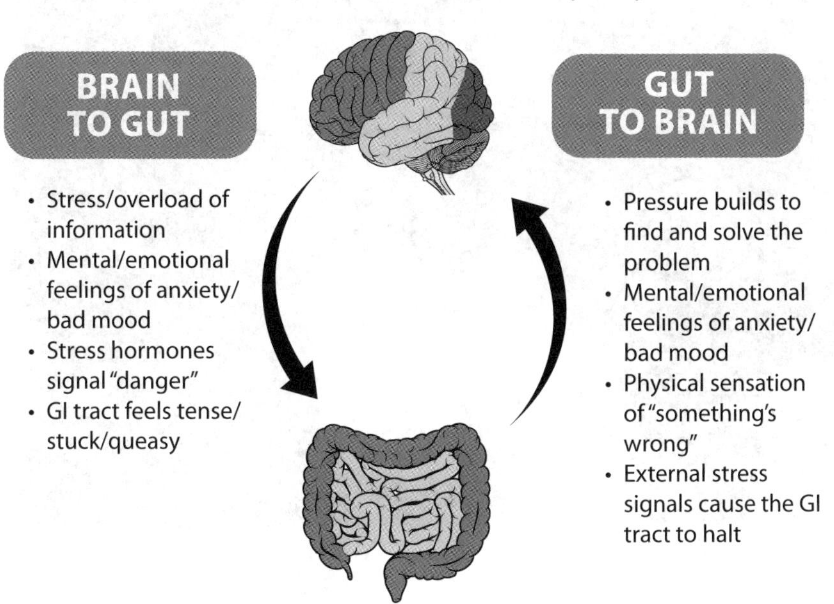

While the brain is indeed the center of information processing, with so much information coming in—light, sound, senses, people, emotions—it can sometimes fail to acknowledge or categorize all that it is receiving. That's why the brain is sometimes dependent on other areas of the body, like the gut, to help it identify that something is important. It's hard to imagine that the stomach can see what's going on in the outside world and then inform the brain. It doesn't have eyes or ears, so how does it receive information? This is where the gut-brain axis comes into play.

* Bravo, J. A., Forsythe, P., Chew, M. V., Escaravage, E., Savignac, H. M., Dinan, T. G., Bienenstock, J., & Cryan, J. F. (2011). Ingestion of *Lactobacillus* strain regulates emotional behavior and central GABA receptor expression in a mouse via the vagus nerve. *Proceedings of the National Academy of Sciences, 108*(38), 16050–16055. https://doi.org/10.1073/pnas.1102999108

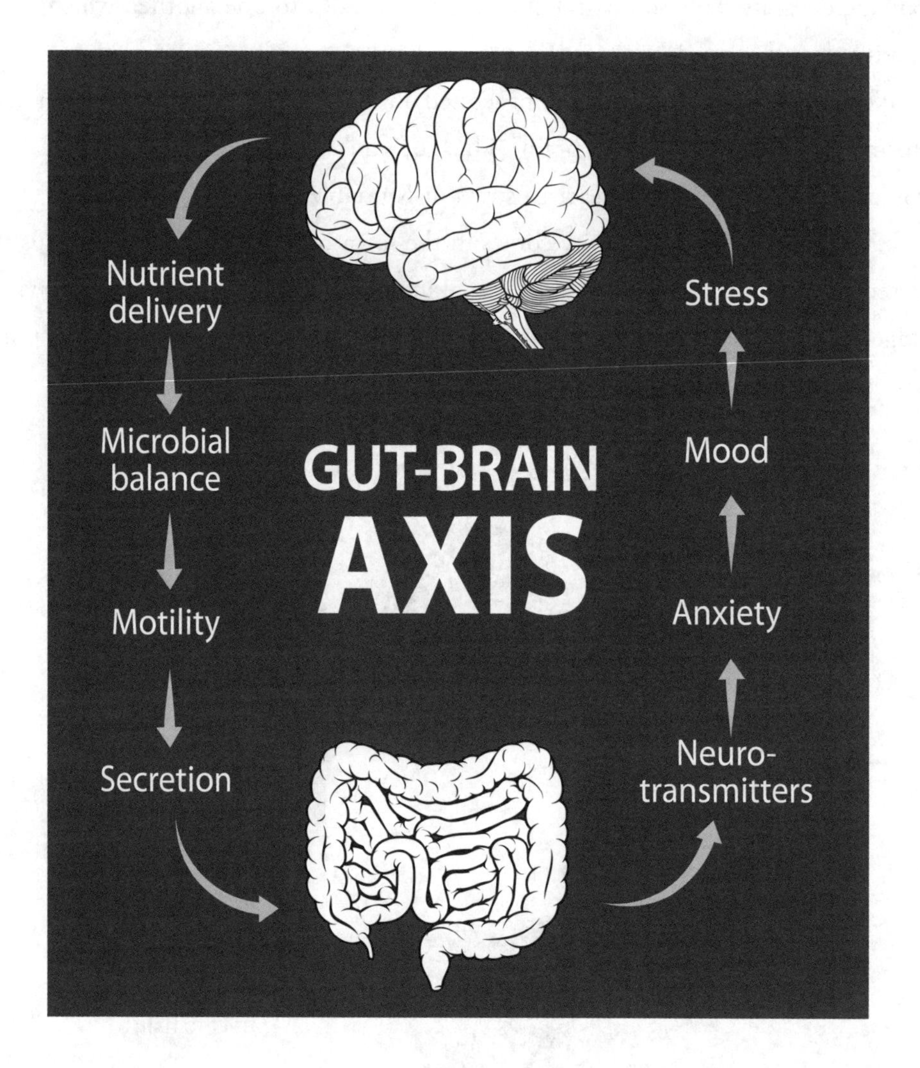

As the illustration shows, sometimes this communication happens in the other direction as well. The brain says to the gut, "I'm overloaded and cannot process all the information I'm getting, so I'm sending you some stress hormones to jar you into realizing it!" These hormones sent to the gut are the reason "gut instinct" occurs. The sick feeling, the butterflies, the feeling of a sudden drop like you're descending in an elevator—all these sensations in the gut are the result of stress hormones sent in reaction to cues in the environment that have not been consciously processed by the brain.

Of course, even when the gut feels something, it doesn't have the capacity to think and make a decision. Instead, it sends stress chemicals up to the brain. Unfortunately, here is where a disconnect can occur. An unaware brain processes this as *Ugh, I feel sick to my stomach*, but it fails to get curious about what may have occurred that contributed to this feeling. Environmental cues are ignored, and the brain carries on as if nothing is happening.

This is what initially occurred with Michael. When he originally walked up to the car and spoke with the kids in the back seat, he visually inspected the back seat and his eyes passed over something on the floorboard, but what it was did not immediately sink in. In other words, he received an environmental cue but didn't consciously process it because his emotional mind was distracted by concern for maintaining the relationships he had built. It was only when he walked away, putting some space between the emotions around dealing with the kids, that his brain was able to fully process again. He recalled to me, "I remember seeing something that was out of place, but I was so caught up in feeling bad about giving this kid a ticket that I didn't process what I saw." Fortunately, when his unconscious mind sent a stress signal that caused his gut to feel uneasy, he decided to pay attention.

TACTICAL BRAIN TRAINING IN ACTION

Scenario: Michael is feeling conflicted about pulling over kids he knows, thus confusing lines of trust and respect. He is distracted by these feelings.

Awareness: He walks away from the car, knowing something is wrong.

Internal Signal: He feels a heavy and uncomfortable feeling in his gut.

Amygdala: Just get back to the squad car so these feelings go away. And send out the stress signals!

PFC: Ticket given. Time to get back to your car. Can't think about anything else!

Mindfulness in Action:

- Awareness: *I am caught up in my emotions regarding ticketing kids I know.*
- Paying attention: *I should pay attention to, and be curious about, what I am feeling right now.*
- Present moment: *I'm noticing a heavy and uncomfortable feeling in my stomach. I have a gut feeling something is wrong.*
- Non-judgmentally: *It doesn't matter that I already walked away, I can walk back and begin again.*

Mindfulness Intervention: *I need to connect with my body, so my brain can start to process information. As I walk back to their car, I will connect the sensation in my stomach. Inhale—"Where do I feel it?" Exhale—"What do I feel?"*

Amygdala: This is upsetting, but it's time to make a plan. Decrease secretion of stress hormones and allow the PFC to think.

PFC: I feel like the gut is alerting me to something I missed. There was a cue that I unconsciously tagged but didn't consciously pick up on. Now that I can think, I recall that I saw something out of place in the back of the car. Let's go investigate.

When Michael went back to the car and looked in the back seat, he saw what he had already seen but had not yet processed: a few bullets lying on the floor. Caught up in his emotions around possibly losing trust with these boys, it was easier for his brain to file this information away in a hidden compartment than to deal with it in the moment. But when this information triggered the distribution of stress hormones to his gut, he incorporated a mindfulness intervention, connecting his thoughts to movement, and allowed his body to help him remember the filed-away information that needed to be looked at.

CONTACT INTERVENTION

Sometimes it's difficult to actually *feel* a body part. You know where it is, you just can't actually feel it. One way to train for this is to practice feeling where a particular body part makes contact with something and then name it. For example, next time you take a shower, let the water hit your back and see if you can feel where the water touches you. Name it—*Back*—then move to your hands. Feel the water on your hand and name it—*Hand*—then move to your face. Feel the water on your eyes, cheeks, nose, lips, and name each contact point. You can do this to your entire body. This helps create neurological connections between identifying a body part and connecting it to a physical sensation. This training cultivates awareness around your felt senses, making you more attuned to bodily discomfort when it arises during real-time interactions.

PRACTICING MINDFULNESS

When we look back on a stressful or reactive situation, questions often come to mind like *Why did that go so poorly?* or *Where did it go wrong?* and even *How did I miss that?* or *I just knew that was going to happen!* This happens because doing things automatically or under stress tends to result in environmental cues being consciously missed, or thoughts, feelings, and sensations going unprocessed. Mindfulness teaches us to listen and notice as the situation (or our reaction to it) is unfolding. Practicing mindfulness develops our ability to attune to our gut feelings, which can then help process cues that our subconscious has picked up on. This allows information to move to the PFC for conscious processing.

Some mindfulness interventions (like the contact intervention just described) work to specifically connect the mind and the physical body. As we practice bringing awareness to different parts of our bodies, the brain improves its ability to connect physical feelings with conscious thinking. This is exactly what Michael was able to accomplish. Michael had a feeling in his gut. When he identified and connected with the feeling that he initially ignored, he was able to move from *feeling* to *thinking* and then take responsive action. Noticing those moments of intuition/gut feeling/instinct/whatever you want to call it can help prompt the executive functioning to jump online and make necessary, time-sensitive decisions.

CONTEMPLATION QUESTIONS

Have you ever acted on a gut feeling?

____

____

____

____

What made you notice that feeling?

____

____

____

____

DON'T FORGET!

Fill out the first column of the self-assessment chart before practicing the mindfulness intervention.

Mindfulness Intervention Self-Assessment

SENSING

The self-assessment chart that follows is designed to track your progress. This chart will help you assess three things:

- How you feel before doing the mindfulness intervention, from 1 = you feel your best to 5 = you feel your worst
- How you feel after doing the mindfulness intervention, from 1 = you feel your best to 5 = you feel your worst
- How you felt while practicing the mindfulness intervention, from 1 = it was pleasant to 5 = it was unpleasant

Fill out the first column of the chart *before* you move on to the mindfulness intervention practice in this chapter. *After* you've practiced the intervention, fill out the second and third columns.

Remember that these assessments are subjective. There are no right or wrong answers and no judgment. And make it easy on yourself—write it down directly in the book, and you can always come back to it for reference.

MINDFULNESS INTERVENTION SELF-ASSESSMENT

Pre-assessment	Post-assessment	Summary Assessment
Overall Mood/Quality (1 = Best → 5 = Worst)	Overall Mood/Quality (1 = Best → 5 = Worst)	Quality of Intervention (1 = Pleasant → 5 = Unpleasant)

Mindfulness Intervention

SENSING

This active practice helps create a connection between feeling a sensation and incorporating purposeful breathing. The training supports tuning into sensations in your body that may already be present but might go unnoticed. When tapping into the sensations and then adding breathing, the mind can move away from stress and focus on whatever task is at hand.

How to Practice

Set a timer for practicing or do what feels comfortable for you.

1. **Find a comfortable position.** Either sit in a way that is comfortable or stand with your feet secure on the ground, about hip width apart. You should have a feeling of sitting or standing tall, in a way that creates a sense of being aware of your surroundings. Keep your eyes open, only closing them if you feel comfortable and balanced.
2. **Place your hands together.** Start with your hands in front of you, touching palm to palm. Then begin to rub both palms together. Slowly increase the speed of movement, building momentum, creating a sense of friction between your hands. Keep building speed, up to your top speed, and then count to 10 while continuing to rub your hands together.
3. **Feel the sensation in your hands.** Now stop moving your hands and open your palms about three to six inches apart from one another. Bring your attention to what you feel in and between your hands. Notice if you feel vibration, tingling, or a sense pulsing in your hands, or even if you feel as if your hands are being pushed away from one another. At this point you can keep your eyes open or close them.
4. **Connect movement to the breath.** Now begin to slowly open your hands wider, about one foot apart, and inhale as you do so. Then exhale as you bring your hands together. Then open your hands even wider,

taking a longer inhale, and close your hands together as you exhale. Continue opening and closing, taking your hands wider and wider with each breath, connecting your breath with movement. Notice what it feels like to breathe and move at the same time. Do this about 10 times.

5. **Place your hands on your legs.** After you have completed what feels comfortable to you, place your hands on your lap. Bring your awareness to your fingers, palms, the backs of your hands, naming each as you do so.
6. **Three closing breaths.** Once you have practiced for a comfortable amount of time, take three deep closing breaths, exhaling longer than inhaling. Bring your attention to your feet on the ground and think about what they feel like. Take one more breath and open your eyes, or just refocus on the room.

Mindfulness Intervention QR Code: Guided Sensing

You can check out a recorded guided practice here:

Mindfulness Intervention Self-Assessment

Return to the self-assessment chart to fill out the postassessment and summary assessment columns *after* you practice the mindfulness intervention.

CHAPTER 14

TRAINING YOUR BRAIN TO THINK

"Look up at the stars and not down at your feet."

– Stephen Hawking

In this chapter, I will address:

- Why first responders are pulled toward the edges of tolerance
- How mindfulness fits into the life of a first responder
- What happens when you hit an edge
- Mindfulness intervention: **Mindful Walking**

RIDING THE EDGES

Why are first responders (and military, medical services, and so many others) pulled toward the edge of tolerance? Most people are taught to protect themselves and avoid danger at all costs, but for a first responder, the exact opposite is the preferable action. The job would not exist were it not for emergencies, so it makes sense that the edge of danger is where the perceived desired action is. Being on high alert and riding the edges all day can feel like purpose and energy, which is helpful when working. But before long, continually living on that edge makes it feel like a normal state of being. This bleeds over from work life and enters personal life. As a result, other feelings like relaxation and calm can feel muted and boring. This can show up as unease and a feeling of being unfulfilled during downtime.

For personalities like this, finding balance in life, taking moments to give back to yourself, and creating happiness can feel awkward. But while stress and chaos undeniably come with the job of a first responder, habituating to and becoming comfortable with that stress and chaos is optional. Being revved up all the time might feel normal, but being effective as a first responder does not require a revved up state each and every moment of life.

I'm not saying it's easy to leave the stress at the scene of the incident or that you shouldn't want to do exciting things during personal time. As I've shared, being the daughter of two first responders meant that walking toward danger and trauma was what we did. This behavior (and action) was ingrained in me from a young age, to the point that I came to categorize it as excitement. My parents constantly lived on the edge of danger, regardless of whether they were on duty or not. It made them good at taking care of business when they were called to a scene of tragedy and chaos. But it also made them crave even more danger, the connected "excitement," and even the hypervigilance and exhaustion that followed. Those feelings were familiar—they felt right, even if they didn't feel good. Suggesting they try acceptance, peace, and contentment would have been like asking someone who doesn't know how to swim to relax in a jacuzzi.

A first responder's job is to run into the fire, chase the bad guy, ask the difficult questions, stay on the phone line through the violence, lean into a car accident, even run toward shots fired. These behaviors are not only taught but reinforced in first responder jobs, regardless of either positive or negative outcomes. As we've seen so many times in previous chapters, chronic exposure to stress builds up over time and leads to both internal unease and external negative reactions. For our family, this showed up as a tendency to overreact to the small things. Showing up late or missing a homework assignment was met with a violent outburst of yelling. For bigger things, like financial difficulty or medical issues, the tendency was to detach and turn inward, ignoring bills or neglecting the need to seek medical care. And given that my parents were working 12-hour shifts, or three days on/two days off, with everyday responsibilities, chores, and homework crammed in between, sleep was more of a concept than a practice.

As noted in previous chapters, the more a behavior is repeated, the more it becomes second nature to perform. Even when you don't consciously enjoy being stressed out, riding the edge all the time cultivates a tendency to lean into stress, as opposed to away from it. The more familiar stress and danger are, the more "comfortable" they become for your brain and body. After all, stress pumps you up, gets the blood flowing, increases adrenaline. By comparison, when things are calm and even-keeled, life may feel dull and boring. When new complications require you to slow down and deliberate with care, it can feel like you aren't doing anything. Riding an edge starts to feel reassuring or even addictive, generating excitement that can make all other behavior and settings pale in comparison. Why slow down or live in the doldrums when a thrilling mission is right there waiting for you?

There is brain science to back this up. A 2004 study suggests that stressful events can be associated with a release in dopamine, the chemical that creates a sense of satisfaction and motivation. Herein lies the problem: If stress is bad but makes you feel good, why would you change? And if we do change our chronic stress state, how can we still have the dopamine dump that our body craves?*

One of the ideas behind TBT is changing the brain's narrative from "stress is exciting" to "balance and happiness is exciting." By creating this new narrative, we can access not only a healthier baseline state of being but also train ourselves for a new experience of healthy excitement. Contrary to what you might assume, this will not lead to inefficiency at work or a laissez-faire attitude toward the real needs and concerns in your life. Rather, it creates a sense of awareness around good stress and bad stress that helps wean us away from reactive or harmful behavior and instead supports behavior that is responsive and constructive, both in our jobs and in our daily lives.

CURATING YOUR CALM

You're probably familiar with the way that rock erodes—not from a single hard-crashing wave, but instead from a small but constant drip, drip, drip that never lets up. Daily stressors have the same effect on the body and mind, causing our physical strength and mental resilience to slowly break down. Since coming face-to-face with daily stressors is an inevitable part of the job for a first responder, it stands to reason that having a go-to strategy for finding emotional balance before, during, and after a hard day (or even just a hard call) is essential to avoid the erosion. Along with stress,

---

* Pruessner, J. C., Champagne, F., Meaney, M. J., & Dagher, A. (2004). Dopamine release in response to a psychological stress in humans and its relationship to early life maternal care: A positron emission tomography study using [^{11}C]raclopride. *Journal of Neuroscience, 24*(11), 2825–2831. https://doi.org/10.1523/JNEUROSCI.3422-03.2004

another inevitable part of the job is change. The first responder's day is filled with the unknown. You can't predict what's behind the door, how bad an accident will be, when you will encounter violence, or how the public will react during an emergency. You also can't predict what will trigger you or at what moment its impact will land.

Part of the objective of offering multiple mindfulness interventions in this book is bringing awareness to the fact that mindfulness is not a one-size-fits-all solution. What worked for Joan may not work for Michael. What worked for Jill may not work for Chief Smith. What works for me may not work for you. That's why it's vital to curate a toolbox filled with a variety of tools that work for you in different situations or moods. It's also worth noting that as you practice the mindfulness interventions, shifts may occur as your comfort increases with the practice itself, changing yet again which tools you resonate with.

Creating a personal strategy can be exciting, offering a journey of self-discovery, growth, and connection to yourself and to others. It can help you break free from cycles of anxiety and overthinking and allow you to take control over your actions and pave the way for a more fulfilling life.

I remember being in kindergarten, standing in a circle with all my school friends as we learned about stop, drop, and roll. We loved this lesson because it meant we could flop down on the ground and roll around, but the fun also taught us something important: If we were ever on fire, we should stop what we were doing, drop to the ground, and roll around to put the fire out. Learning the process before it was needed helped train our brains for recall, if and when there was a need for implementation.

This process also works well as a prompt for stress and trauma management. Having a plan of action is key to putting out the mental/emotional "fire" and preventing or mitigating its damage. Here's how it works for TBT. You feel like something is not right (stress, trauma, overwhelm, sadness, distraction, freeze state):

- **STOP** and listen to what the warning signals and your body are telling you
- **DROP** into awareness and assess what could work to help regulate your nervous system
- **ROLL** into a mindfulness intervention that works for you and for the situation

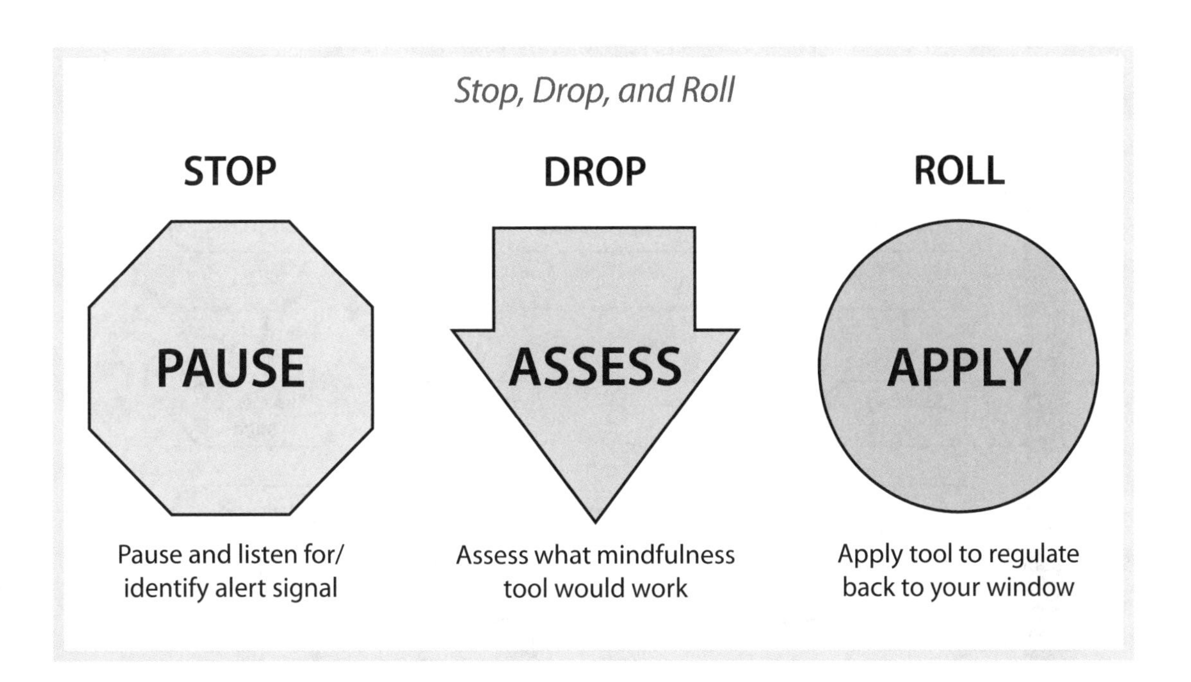
Stop, Drop, and Roll
STOP
DROP
ROLL
PAUSE
ASSESS
APPLY
Pause and listen for/ identify alert signal
Assess what mindfulness tool would work
Apply tool to regulate back to your window

Which Mindfulness Intervention?

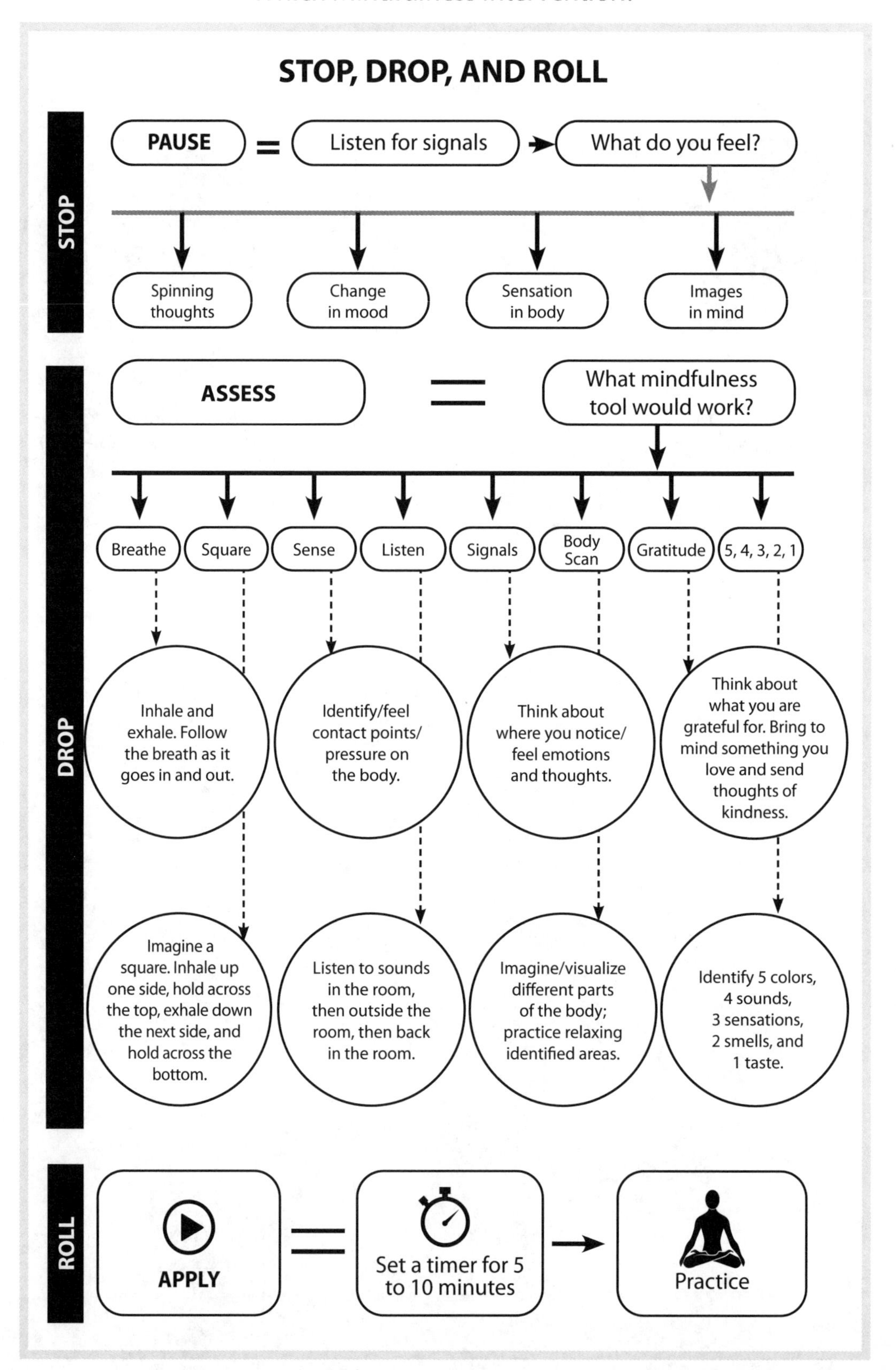

WHY NOT TRAIN TO FEEL GOOD?

Mindfulness can be boiled down to three words: **present-moment awareness**. While considering the past is relevant for contemplating happy memories or analyzing an incident for what worked and what didn't, and future thinking is great for planning your life or anticipating something around the corner, the present moment—what is occurring in this moment, right now, where you currently reside mentally and physically—is the only moment that matters in terms of contentment and life balance.

Training to support present-moment awareness means training for the moment that matters most: this one. Within this moment—this very moment in which you're reading this paragraph—you can feel a lot of ways. You can feel excited about the opportunity to learn. Or you can feel frustrated that this isn't all easy to process. Or you can feel distracted . . . yes, even as you're actively trying to cultivate present-moment awareness! Acknowledging whatever you're feeling is the first step. The second step is moving toward something that serves you.

So which emotional experience *is* the most beneficial for you? To some degree, it's situationally dependent—if you're pulling up to your daughter's birthday party, feeling joyful and excited is probably the most beneficial emotion to bring to the situation. You're going to help everyone have a better time if you're having a great time. If you're pulling up to a tragic car accident, joy and excitement aren't quite on the mark, but neither are devastation and frustration. Arriving on the scene with feelings of *What the bleep is wrong with drivers in this area?* or *Why is the world so cruel?* does not serve you or the people you're trying to help. What does help is showing up with emotional balance—you recognize the severity of the situation, you have empathy for the people involved, you are confident (and maybe even a little pumped) about being there because you're trained to manage the situation, and you have a sense of peace and acceptance that whatever the outcome, you'll have done your utmost to be of service. I often describe this feeling with the word "copacetic," but a more casual way of saying it might be **contentment**.

Contentment doesn't mean living in a blissed-out cloud of positivity or chanting "om" as you go through your workday. Rather, contentment is fundamentally about experiencing deliberate emotions in the moment through the filter of a regulated nervous system. When your own nervous system is well managed, it has a mirror effect on others that helps them manage their own emotional states. It also helps keep you grounded in the midst of the inevitable adrenaline rush, improving your ability to make split-second decisions and deal with new factors as they pop up. TBT helps cultivate a baseline of contentment, protecting you from the sudden drop in adrenaline and dopamine (and the connected feelings of numbness, anxiety, or depression) that can hit once you leave the situation. Finally, instead of itching for the next emergency to flood your system with dopamine, you're training for a steady drip of feel-good chemicals that come from living in emotional balance and taking care of your nervous system.

Bottom line, along with creating more ease in your own life, contentment helps you interact more effectively with danger, suffering, and chaos. If you can bring a baseline of contentment to an emergent situation, you're bringing a host of other attributes—confidence, calm, compassion, hope—that can influence the situation for the better. As strange as it might sound, cultivating contentment is extremely valuable for the people you serve. It helps with managing job-related trauma, fosters an acceptance of the unpredictability of the job, helps support mental resilience, and makes it possible to leave the trauma at work so you can be present for the people you love.

It's true that being content can take work. However, doing that work in itself makes you content. We talked in chapter 11 about the back-and-forth effect of the first responder role: You get knocked down, you come back up, you get knocked down again. Training for contentment decreases the length of time you spend between those two points.

Living on the extreme edges is not safe or healthy for you, personally or professionally. It doesn't contribute to effectiveness at your job nor to peace at home. It's emotionally and physically exhausting to alternate between the highs of dopamine rush and the crash of dopamine deficiency. It's fatiguing, it breaks down your immune system, it makes it difficult to function in life, much less enjoy it. Cultivating contentment and emotional balance brings a sense of ease and comfort that offers a buffer against the blows of this job and makes it easier to enjoy the safety that you've helped create for others. The whole objective of the first responder job is to restore safety, health, order, normalcy—I would argue this is incumbent not only for the victims of the situation but also for yourself.

CONTEMPLATION QUESTIONS

Do you notice a desire to run toward danger?

____

____

____

____

Can you imagine using mindfulness interventions to notice your edges?

____

____

____

____

DON'T FORGET!

Fill out the first column of the self-assessment chart before practicing the mindfulness intervention.

Mindfulness Intervention Self-Assessment

MINDFUL WALKING

The self-assessment chart that follows is designed to track your progress. This chart will help you assess three things:

- How you feel before doing the mindfulness intervention, from 1 = you feel your best to 5 = you feel your worst
- How you feel after doing the mindfulness intervention, from 1 = you feel your best to 5 = you feel your worst
- How you felt while practicing the mindfulness intervention, from 1 = it was pleasant to 5 = it was unpleasant

Fill out the first column of the chart *before* you move on to the mindfulness intervention practice in this chapter. *After* you've practiced the intervention, fill out the second and third columns.

Remember that these assessments are subjective. There are no right or wrong answers and no judgment. And make it easy on yourself—write it down directly in the book, and you can always come back to it for reference.

MINDFULNESS INTERVENTION SELF-ASSESSMENT

Pre-assessment	Post-assessment	Summary Assessment
Overall Mood/Quality (1 = Best → 5 = Worst)	Overall Mood/Quality (1 = Best → 5 = Worst)	Quality of Intervention (1 = Pleasant → 5 = Unpleasant)

Mindfulness Intervention

MINDFUL WALKING

This practice will help you connect with your body. It is especially useful in moments when things feel dull or boring, or when it feels difficult to sit still. A walking meditation is an active practice that can help reduce anxiety and calm the mind.

How to Practice

Set a timer for practicing or do what feels comfortable for you.

1. **Find a location.** Walking can be done indoors or outdoors, but if you have an opportunity to walk outdoors, take it! You can even do this practice anytime you are walking, such as at the grocery store or on the way to your car.
2. **Notice your body.** Begin by standing still and noticing your feet on the ground. Take a slow, deep breath and set your gaze on what's in front of you.
3. **Walk forward slowly.** Walk 10 to 15 paces forward at slightly slower than your normal pace. Notice the feeling of your feet on the ground and the sensations involved in walking. If an impulse to move quickly arises, notice it and continue forward at a slow pace.
4. **Breathe with every step.** Focus your attention on your inhales and exhales as you walk. With each step, try to repeat in your mind *Step, step, step*. If you notice your mind becomes distracted, gently guide your awareness back to your breath.
5. **Notice your movement.** Notice the sensation of your body as you move. First notice your foot touching the ground, then lift it off the ground, and finally return it to the ground again. Move slowly and purposefully. Repeat in your mind *Right foot, left foot, right foot, left foot*.
6. **Turn around.** At the end of 10 to 15 paces, come to a stopping place and take a slow breath. Then turn around and walk back using the

same process. Continue like this for 10 to 15 minutes, or as long as is comfortable.

Mindfulness Intervention QR Code: Guided Mindful Walking

You can check out a recorded guided practice here:

Mindfulness Intervention Self-Assessment

Return to the self-assessment chart to fill out the postassessment and summary assessment columns *after* you practice the mindfulness intervention.

CHAPTER 15

HOW TO START A PRACTICE

"The most beautiful experience we can have is the mysterious. It is the fundamental emotion that stands at the cradle of true art and science."

– Albert Einstein

In this chapter, I will address:

- How to make mindfulness sustainable
- The importance of practice
- How to create a mindfulness practice
- Mindfulness intervention: **Body Scan**

THE THREEFOLD APPROACH

Growing up in California, I remember earthquake drills as a frequent occurrence during my years in school. We were taught to hide under our desks or step into a doorway to protect ourselves from falling walls or a ceiling caving in. Today, kids are taught active shooter drills in school, including how to make the decision to barricade, fight, or run. Learning what to do about a potential danger helps us create a strategy for when that particular event occurs. This is also true for assessing an event after the fact: You can look back and establish what you would do differently in the future. Stress, however, is never just one incident or one person or one event. It can be very specific, yes, and it can also feel very elusive. In order to have an effective tactical stress-management plan, strategies must be learned and applied on a wide range of issues, across a wide range of activities. It isn't only about analyzing the traumatic case last week, or preparing for the upcoming assignment next week, or even tolerating the annoying coworker sitting next to you. To make it stick, TBT must be applied at every stage of an incident—before, during, and after—in every moment at home, and in every moment on the job.

In our house, we did not have a lot of home-cooked meals. When I would go to a friend's house for dinner, I was always excited to come home and try to recreate it. I found that it's easy to sit down and eat a meal, but it can be a little overwhelming to hop in the kitchen and make a meal that tastes good, is good for you, and is easy to prepare.

In the same way, the stories shared on these pages are meant to give you a taste of what it's like for first responders (and others working in high-trauma environments) to use mindfulness tools before, during, or after a critical event to create a better outcome for themselves and the people they serve. Sometimes, though, these tools are easier to conceptualize than to actually implement. So how do you go from concept to application? How do you build and maintain a mindfulness practice that works?

The answer lies in following a threefold approach:

- First, TBT focuses on **understanding** why these goals are important and why these tools are needed to reach them. Understanding the *why* helps create awareness surrounding how the body regulates stress, how it processes emotional balance, and what happens when it pops out of the window of tolerance.
- Second, TBT asks us to **assess** which approach works best for each of us. This means assessing not only which mindfulness intervention resonates for you but also which one is appropriate for a given situation. Would taking three breaths calm your nervous system or activate it? Does listening to sounds create anxiety, or does it help you focus? Practicing different mindfulness interventions in different situations helps us establish our best personal fit for specific circumstances and needs. The better we know which tools serve us, the more easily we can manage our triggers and emotions and bounce back from a hyper- or hypovigilant state, enabling us to find happiness, which then helps us get the job done!

- Third, TBT provides a framework for **implementing** your personalized strategy. The word "mindfulness" translates from a word in Pali meaning "that which we remember." The more we train, the easier it becomes to remember the steps needed to calm the nervous system: Pause, listen to what's happening internally, then take an action that serves you. TBT directs us back to the previously laid path so that we can follow it in the moment of emergency and navigate back to safety. Practicing a mindfulness intervention under relaxed conditions builds this capacity for reflective thinking, allowing us to remember what to do in the moments when it matters.

WHY PRACTICE IS ESSENTIAL

As we discussed in the last chapter, mindfulness is definitely not a one-size-fits-all application. You have experimented with a handful of mindfulness interventions over the course of this book. Some worked for you, some didn't . . . and that's normal. The idea behind offering different approaches is to find what works in your life, establish a system that serves you, and practice it over and over and over again—before you get up to start your day, after an argument, while taking a shower, in the middle of a traumatic incident, before you go to bed, and even while driving (please don't close your eyes to practice!). Again, the more you practice a behavior, the stronger that behavior becomes. The more you practice mindfulness, the more likely you are to make it a part of your everyday life. When a situation triggers you as a perceived emergency, you can easily self-correct. When an actual emergency arises, you are better prepared to respond and even to pivot if necessary.

The neurological pathways ingrained from previous practice become stronger with each repetition. This makes the mindfulness interventions more efficient each time you implement them, whether in an emergency situation or in everyday life. Practicing also helps build confidence and a better understanding of the efficacy of each intervention. The familiarity you develop acts as a positive reinforcement—remember, your brain interprets "familiar" as safe and comfortable—which develops a desire to practice even more.

Here's a simple and effective way to begin:

- Week 1: Start with a five-minute practice, two to three times a day.
- Week 2: Transition to a 10-minute practice, two times a day.
- Week 3: If you like practicing two times a day, continue to do so and add more time to one or both. Or you can decrease to one time per day and increase the time to a 15-minute practice.
- Week 4: Choose your own adventure!

The following template can be copied for use in your weekly mindfulness training. Practice with a specific plan one week at a time. Play with time and frequency over subsequent weeks and see what works. You can always change this as you progress or, if you feel like things aren't sitting right, you can begin again with the five-minute practice time. There is no "right" way to practice. It's an individualized approach based on your schedule, your desire, your situation.

MINDFULNESS TRAINING PLAN

	Morning	Afternoon	Evening
Example:	Breathing Meditation (5 minutes)	Mindful Walk (5 minutes)	Body Scan (5 minutes)
MON			
TUE			
WED			
THU			
FRI			
SAT			
SUN			

IT'S PERSONAL

One of the key constructs of TBT is the ability to personalize the strategy, planning, and execution of managing stress and trauma. Creating a personalized approach can be highly effective in that it allows the tailoring of specific goals and needs. Picking and choosing which mindfulness intervention best fits your personality and lifestyle helps establish a connection to the interventions themselves, as well as create a more accessible training.

To create a personalized approach, self-analysis is necessary. Look back at each self-assessment chart and reflect on how each mindfulness intervention felt for you, or what it brought up, or how well it helped you regulate your emotions. Choose the ones you most resonated with and fill in the table that follows with an achievable weekly plan. Start small, and slowly build over time. You can also supplement the mindfulness interventions listed in this book with meditation apps, online guided meditations, or other meditations you know. Be curious, and experiment with what works best for you.

STRENGTH CAN COME FROM STRUGGLE

I once read a story about a boy finding a chrysalis hanging in a tree. He speculated that it was housing a caterpillar waiting to become a butterfly. As he was looking at it, it began to move, and he realized whatever was inside was struggling to get out. Wanting to help, he ran home, got his pocketknife, and proceeded to cut a small slit in the chrysalis to help the insect's progress. As the slit he created widened and opened, a beautiful butterfly quickly emerged. It opened its wings and began to take flight. Just as suddenly, it dropped to the ground, unable to fly. The boy ran home and told his mother what had happened. She then explained that what he had interpreted as a struggle was in fact a purposeful part of the butterfly's growth. By pushing on the internal walls of the chrysalis, the butterfly was growing and building its wing strength. Only through this struggle could it build the strength to eventually fly.

The same can be said for practicing mindfulness interventions. Even sitting down for the 10 minutes it takes to do a mindfulness intervention can sometimes feel like pushing against a concrete wall. Compared to the discomfort of these new thoughts and feelings, it's easy to feel like you'd rather do anything else instead, even fight with your spouse about nothing or eat your way through the refrigerator at 3:00 a.m. But just as with the training you underwent to become a first responder, it's the struggle that builds the strength. As your mindfulness practice progresses, you develop more and more strategies to help you sit for a few more seconds, take a few more breaths, spend a little more get-to-know-you time with these new healthy sensations. Persevering through discomfort during a mindfulness intervention organizes the mind around the idea of allowing discomfort to exist, rather than pushing against it. This training informs the brain that discomfort itself is not a bad thing when you have strategies for managing it. Sound like something that could be helpful when you're knee-deep in chaos, danger, and human suffering?

TBT teaches us to recognize that we are in control of our own destiny. It does so by giving us access to purposefully made choices, agency, and free will. When stressed or feeling overwhelmed, rather than walking down the same road (and falling into the same hole), we can change course: Notice that you are upset, sad, or stressed, then make a conscious choice on how you want to interact. Do you need to step away for a moment, take a walk, do some deep breathing, read a book, take a hot shower? Be curious, and then choose. That's free will. That's mindfulness.

BEGINNER'S MIND

Throughout this book, we've practiced a variety of mind-body interventions. Our final intervention, the **Body Scan**, brings together feelings, sensations, and thoughts with what we've learned about redirecting when feelings are intense to something that is soothing and grounding and restores ease in the body and mind. Sometimes we don't even know that we're holding tension in our shoulders, jaw, or fists. We're unknowingly triggered, and our body and brain respond protectively. The Body Scan is not only informative but also prescriptive—it lets you know you're holding tension and where, then trains you to relax those places in order to deal with the tension, rather than stashing it away where you can ignore it.

Somehow, we've received the message that the solution for stress and overwhelm is to "just relax." Oftentimes, though, trying to simply relax the body creates more stress. If we don't know how to recognize what mental/emotional stress feels like in the body and redirect our thoughts and feelings to something soothing, it can generate more tension, more anxiety, more depression. Instead, learning what information our minds and bodies hold before pivoting to relaxation is all it takes to help us truly redirect and eventually release pent-up tension, even tension we didn't know we were carrying.

Just as during stressful moments it can be unclear what's occurring emotionally and physically, it can also be unclear when or even how to apply mindfulness strategies when we need them the most. This is all so normal, and it's all part of the process. One interesting aspect of mindfulness is its emphasis on something we touched on back in chapter 8: the **beginner's mind**.

The beginner's mind involves approaching life, situations, people, and even the practice of mindfulness itself with a sense of wonder and curiosity. While it is great to be an expert, it can also be very limiting. Once you know everything, where else is there to go? The expert has nothing new to learn. The mind of a beginner, on the other hand, has the world to explore. Approaching a task, the public, or a victim with a beginner's mind can help reduce the mental burden associated with assuming one already knows all the answers. Rather, it offers an opportunity to look at the situation for what it is and be curious about it. Just the act of being curious and asking questions gives you agency to act or respond in a conscious, constructive way.

This is as true at the scene of a house fire or a car accident as it is when dealing with a toddler's tantrum or even your own complicated thoughts and emotions.

And yes, sometimes asking questions is uncomfortable, or incorporating an intervention can feel awkward. Even here, being curious about the discomfort you're feeling is the key. Rather than working to disappear the discomfort, you can change your view of it and embrace it.

After going through intense training to become a first responder, you know by now that feeling uncomfortable is not necessarily a bad thing. The idea of discomfort can actually be flipped, taking you from feeling bad excitement to feeling good excitement, from unease to challenge. Confronting a challenge is how growth occurs. By doing things that make us uncomfortable, we expand our comfort zone and, with it, our window of tolerance. Through simply being curious about what you are feeling, what you are sensing, what you are seeing, the nervous system calms down a bit, allowing a moment of reprieve from the uncomfortable feeling. Creating this space between what is occurring and how you will relate to it allows you to be with the uncomfortable feeling just a bit longer. Yes, something may be unsettling, but you made it through anyway.

In short, the beginner's mind often has the outcome of changing your relationship with what is occurring. Curiosity allows you to work with an adverse situation, rather than against it, and even increase your own boundaries for what's comfortable and manageable. First responders are asked to not only have critical thinking skills but also be able to think creatively on the spot. This brings us to the idea of rigid versus flexible thinking. **Rigid thinking** creates the sense that there's only one way to manage a situation. This naturally limits our options, leading to frustration and overwhelm. **Flexible thinking**, on the other hand, frees us up with a sense of variety and options, which leads to the feeling of being relaxed, adaptable, and agile—all things that make first responders effective at their jobs.

CURIOSITY CREATES CALM

There is a certain type of person who walks confidently toward chaos, even when everything else is falling apart around them. We need this in our communities. Ensuring our collective safety and wellness is what makes it possible for parents to feel a sense of assurance when their teen borrows the car at night, for homeowners to leave town for a vacation, for commuters to brave the rush hour freeway, and for weekend warriors to take on ocean waves and mountain trails. Our everyday lives wouldn't be what they are without the vigilance and care of people who run toward chaos. Without first responders, our world would spiral down the drain of entropy.

The same is true for first responders themselves—faced with constant high stress and frequently traumatic experiences, the life of a first responder tends toward entropy. Running toward chaos can be very important, even lifesaving, during an emergency. But as a way of life, it will ultimately run you down. That's why it's essential that first responders learn to take care of themselves just as vigilantly as they take care of the rest of us.

Mindfulness is not saying avoid the chaos. It's saying run toward it with a grounded sense of agency over how you manage both the outcome of the situation and your own internal outcome. TBT offers tools to prepare you before the storm, keep you cool during the commotion, and calm your nervous system when the dust settles.

Training yourself to create order and safety in a scene of disorder and chaos can save lives. Training your own brain to create order out of mental and emotional disorder can change your own life. Be curious and see for yourself. You may find that it's just what you need to find calm within the chaos.

CONTEMPLATION QUESTIONS

What mindfulness interventions do you most resonate with?

____

____

____

____

____

What are a few ways in which mindfulness might help you in your life?

____

____

____

____

____

What are a few ways in which mindfulness can support you in your work?

____

____

____

____

____

DON'T FORGET!

Fill out the first column of the self-assessment chart before practicing the mindfulness intervention.

Mindfulness Intervention Self-Assessment

BODY SCAN

The self-assessment chart that follows is designed to track your progress. This chart will help you assess three things:

- How you feel before doing the mindfulness intervention, from 1 = you feel your best to 5 = you feel your worst
- How you feel after doing the mindfulness intervention, from 1 = you feel your best to 5 = you feel your worst
- How you felt while practicing the mindfulness intervention, from 1 = it was pleasant to 5 = it was unpleasant

Fill out the first column of the chart *before* you move on to the mindfulness intervention practice in this chapter. *After* you've practiced the intervention, fill out the second and third columns.

Remember that these assessments are subjective. There are no right or wrong answers and no judgment. And make it easy on yourself—write it down directly in the book, and you can always come back to it for reference.

MINDFULNESS INTERVENTION SELF-ASSESSMENT

Pre-assessment	Post-assessment	Summary Assessment
Overall Mood/Quality (1 = Best → 5 = Worst)	Overall Mood/Quality (1 = Best → 5 = Worst)	Quality of Intervention (1 = Pleasant → 5 = Unpleasant)

Mindfulness Intervention

BODY SCAN

This practice activates the connection between your mind and body. It will help you identify what your body needs and does not need to thrive. By focusing on different parts of your body during the practice, you can strengthen the link between physical and emotional states of awareness. This can help bring awareness to (and even reduce) real-time stress, anxiety, and physical pain.

How to Practice

Set a timer for practicing or do what feels comfortable for you.

1. **Find a comfortable position.** You can practice this meditation seated or lying down. Come to a position that allows you to relax without falling asleep. Side note: You may fall asleep, and that is okay. This is a great practice to do at the end of the day as a way of relaxing.
2. **Notice your body.** Allow your eyes to close and bring your awareness to your body. Notice the sensation of your body on the floor or the weight of your body on a chair, couch, or bed.
3. **Release any tension in your body.** Inhale and exhale a few times. With every exhale, allow your body to soften and relax.
4. **Bring your attention to different places in your body.** Progressively move from the bottom of your feet to the top of your head. Begin by noticing where your feet make contact with whatever you are on, sensing whether they feel heavy or soft. Move your awareness up your legs: first your ankles, then your calves, then your knees, then your thighs. As you move from one location to the next, notice/feel any tension in each body part. As you do so, inhale, relaxing that part of your body as you exhale. Notice your calf, inhale, then exhale as you soften your calf muscle. Continue like this through your entire body, from your legs to your hips, belly, back, arms, hands and fingers,

shoulders and chest, all the way through to your neck, face, and top of your head. Notice the sensations (temperature, tension, tingling) and allow each part of your body to relax with each exhale. Take as much time with this process as you can—it can take up to 30 minutes, or even longer if desired.

5. **Closing body scan.** After you have completed progressive relaxation through every body part, do a mental scan of your body and notice where you may still be feeling any tension. Once located, take three breaths, exhaling into relaxation. Take one more breath and open your eyes as you exhale.

Mindfulness Intervention QR Code: Guided Body Scan

You can check out a recorded guided practice here:

Mindfulness Intervention Self-Assessment

Return to the self-assessment chart to fill out the postassessment and summary assessment columns *after* you practice the mindfulness intervention.

ACKNOWLEDGMENTS

I cannot express enough thanks to my family and friends for their continued support and encouragement throughout this process.

To my children, Logan, Payson, Verveine, and Hartley (bonus daughter): You inspire me to show up in the world in a way that makes you proud.

To my sisters, Alisa, Brooke, Amber, and Megan, my niece Zan, and sister-in-law Jen: I channeled your brilliance and strength in every word. Your successes keep me motivated and driven.

To my late (bonus) mom, Tina: You taught me to keep pushing through, no matter what.

To Kelly (friend, coparent, and so much more): Thank you for your kindness and for our beautiful family.

To my nephews, Trey, Haden, Sam, and Thomas: Thank you for being interested in my work.

To all my brothers-in-law—Dave, Doc, Mark, Matt—and son-in-law, Ben: Thank you for your curiosity and inquisitive questions.

To the cousin crew—Denise, Bill, Ashley, and Hailey: Our family Zooms have kept me excited about connection.

To my Florida family—Sandy, Heidi, Marina, and Mary: Thank you for the support from afar.

To Lesley University, my graduate advisor Nancy Waring, and my Lesley peers: You laid the foundation of all this work and launched me on an incredible journey.

To PESI Publishing (especially Chelsea and Kayla): Thank you for taking a chance on me, and for all the emails and Zooms and rewrites! Your patience is appreciated.

To Claude Robinson for his amazing videography skills and editing skills in recording the inaugural mindfulness intervention videos.

To my friends who chose book titles, read manuscripts, celebrated with me, and cheered me on: *Thank you.* Your belief in me helped me believe in myself.

To all the first responders and first responder–adjacent medical workers and veterans: Thank you for all that you do. Our world needs you and appreciates you. And to all those I have worked with directly: I have learned so much from you. Thank you for allowing me to share your chronicles with readers. Your experiences help show what is possible.

Finally, to my caring, loving, and supportive husband, Jeff: You've always been my greatest advocate, offering unwavering support. Your presence is my pillar, offering security and a profound sense of safety. Your confidence in my abilities never wavers. My heartfelt gratitude, appreciation, and love go to you.

ABOUT THE AUTHOR

Gina Rollo White, MA, is the founder of Mindful Junkie and is broadly recognized as a leading therapeutic mindfulness expert and instructor for first responders and veterans, teaching stress and trauma management using mindfulness interventions. She provides in-agency and in-department workshops across the US using the curriculum she developed. Tactical Brain Training®, Mindfulness for First Responders. She is also a speaker at major first responder conferences across the country, such as International Association of Chiefs of Police, COG Fire Health and Safety Symposium, Southwest Women in Law Enforcement, and Washington DC, Grand Rounds. She lives in the Washington DC, area.